PENNY STOCK INVESTING
&
ALGORITHMIC TRADING

2-in-1 Compilation

*Generate Profits from Trading Penny Stocks &
Financial Machine Learning With Minimal Risk
and Without Technical Jargon*

Investors Press

Table of Contents

PENNY STOCK INVESTING

ALGORITHMIC TRADING

PENNY STOCK INVESTING

Step-by-Step Guide to Generate Profits from Trading Penny Stocks in as Little as 30 Days with Minimal Risk and Without Drowning in Technical Jargon

by Investors Press

Introduction

The world of trading is vast and daunting. It might even be too expensive. Or that is generally how it is perceived. But what if someone were to tell you that you could invest in a company share for less than two dollars? What if someone told you that you could buy shares for even one dollar? Most people would think you were crazy, but this is where a secret and amazing market comes to light. Penny stock investing is the perfect market for people who may have tighter budgets but who also want to get into the world of trading.

However, if you don't know much about penny stock trading, the big question for you may be, *where do I start?* Well, this book will be your guide! Follow this journey of explanations, facts, tips, and tricks that will act as your guide in the jungle of trading penny stock. You might think that this is the same as all the rest of stock trading, but that is absolutely wrong. Instead, there will be a different approach that you'll have to take, and we'll get into the details and show you how.

From strategies you can consider implementing to instructions on how to research effectively, this guide will help you enter into a much cheaper but still rewarding trading platform. There is great potential in penny stock trading, which is why many other companies invest in them. So why not dip your own toes into the marketing sector, and work on potentially growing your income in ways you have never even thought possible?

Later on, you will also learn about the different forms of chart strategies, as well as how to stay safe from scammers and even more. It might even have a few blunt truths that may surprise you, but all in all, it will be an incredibly rewarding journey. At the end of this book, you will have a vital foundational knowledge that can kick-start your journey into investing in penny stocks and learning how to start growing your income even today. As you get more answers and learn more from the lessons, what might have seemed crazy to you at first can now come true, as there are so many businesses available for you to flourish from. All you need is some determination, basic business knowledge, and a great willingness to learn both from here and from those around you. This is not the only source for penny stock investing, but it is a sure-fire way to get you a jumpstart into this journey. You don't have to be scared either, as everyone must start from somewhere. Being a beginner is not altogether a bad thing. It can mean that you will be more willing to take the necessary steps to gather information and research, rather than just dashing into trading blindly and coming out far worse than you started.

In fact, just the fact that you are reading this is making you far wiser than the average investor, who might just like to try their luck on the trading field. And on average, most of them are not so lucky.

If you want to start trading, even as a beginner, find out all you need right here, without having to spend an excessive amount of money on extensive courses or resources. Although penny stock investing has a lot of information surrounding it, it is not as complicated as people try to make it out to be. In fact, the entire world of trading can be complex at times, but really, you just have to learn the essential information, and the more that you know, the better off you will be for it.

Who Is Investors Press?

Investors Press is a group of professionals who are inspired to help individuals that are looking to start their trading journey. With an extensive amount of research and knowledge on trading stocks, we want to share everything that you will need to get started. We have been formulating a thorough and detailed guide to lead beginners and people who are just looking for a refresher on the basics and on the different aspects of investing in penny stocks. We want to help you achieve your financial goals by teaching you step-by-step lessons on how to build an additional stream of income. Your success matters deeply to us, and we hope this guide can lead you on your way to a greater path of trading. We are here to remove the often hampering reliance you may have on stockbrokers, or other unreliable resources, who have shaded the truth with their own marketing tactics, leading up to inevitable failure. This is exactly what we would like you to avoid. And although mistakes are bound to be made, this book will give you an unbiased viewpoint towards penny stock investing, which is exactly what you will need as a beginner.

Chapter 1:
What Exactly Are Penny Stocks?

In the world of investments, everyone tends to think big, such as expensive shares, thirty-story buildings, and multi-million-dollar companies. But, unfortunately, there are many misconceptions that arise when it comes to investing too. Whether it is the reality that only the rich can invest or all shares are costly. However, investing is most certainly not how the movies tend to portray them (i.e., people standing with a glass of wine talking about shares and being rich).

What if we were to tell you that this is not always the case? That, within the surface of investments, lies a deeper truth about how people could earn money? This is where penny stocks come in. They are a different approach from traditional stock investments and may be just what you need in the investment world.

Definition of Penny Stocks

What exactly are penny stocks? Obviously, they are not stocks sold in mere pennies but are a reference to their low price. According to the US Securities and Exchange Commission (SEC), they are normally called "microcap stock" or penny stock. These are normally associated with companies that have a capitalization of less than $250 million or even $300 million. Some businesses certainly have significantly less capital, as they were always intended to be smaller. However, there are even some companies that go below $50 million, and they are typically referred to as "nano cap stocks."

Naturally, the businesses that have smaller capital will be selling shares at a lower price. Penny stocks are normally sold for under five dollars a share. Although it is possible to use exchanges such as the New York Stock Exchange (NYSE) for penny stock trading, the most popular exchanges for penny stocks will be over-the-counter (OTC) transactions. You get these through the electronic OTC Bulletin Board (OTCBB) or even OTC Market Groups that are privately owned (writer et al., 2021).

Penny stocks used to be traded for less than a dollar. However, considering inflation, the SEC tailored it to mean shares that are below five dollars. This matters because it is up to the SEC to protect investors and create equality and fairness on the investor's platform. But it does mean those bad investment choices will still be listed on the SEC, and every so often, scammers do still slip through the cracks. This is a sad but realistic truth, as much as a person would love to have a singular reliable source to trust. But in this modern-day economy, the life of an investor is full of potential; they just have a lot more they will need to learn.

OTC Markets

If you want to have better access to penny stocks, you would probably want to subscribe to the OTCBB. This happens to be a digital or electronic quotation service that was launched and is run by the Financial Industry Regulatory Authority (FINRA). They give you access to the data and quotes of the OTC markets. But be careful about all the offers and specials they may shoot your way; it is best to stay vigilant, especially when you are using this platform.

The reason why you normally cannot find penny stocks on the big exchanges is because they tend to be more volatile and unlikely to meet the requirements to be listed on the big exchanges. Therefore, if you are interested, it would be best to turn your attention to the platforms where you can find penny stocks. However, be careful as a beginner, as penny stocks are not on the normal exchanges, they tend to have increased chances of failing.

How Do Penny Stocks Differ from Regular Stocks?

Although penny stocks do count as regular stocks to a certain degree, a person cannot deny the differences between the smaller shares and the larger shares, as they are even trading on different platforms. The biggest difference between penny stocks and stocks with higher prices is that it takes a lot more effort and work to discover information on the penny stocks. This gets a little harder, especially because you will need to ensure that the information is reliable, as well as up to date. It is hardly worth investing in something over news that has been shared five years ago. In fact, even two years is pushing it. This is because penny stocks do not garner much attention, and they are not required to register with the SEC. This means penny stocks are less likely to be as regulated when it comes to information. A lot of professional stock analysts happen to write about larger public companies, as it is quite easy to find the information necessary. But the same can certainly not be said about penny stocks, so even finding proper professional opinions on a specific form of penny stock may be a more significant struggle.

This means that if you want to become a savvy penny stock investor, you will need to put in extra work, time, and effort in order to get a hold of good and reliable information. This is needed so that you can make the best and most strategic investment decisions. On the other hand, some larger investments, although risky, are easier to navigate when it comes to finding out the necessary information.

When it comes to penny stocks, they normally come at a higher risk than those that are higher priced. Companies that do want to have their stocks listed on specific exchanges are supposed to meet certain standards, such as a total minimum amount of assets or a minimum number of shareholders. Therefore, they can be considered as a certain number of securities that are truly required for the exchange. This way, investors can hold more confidence in the company just because it managed to make it to the exchange. However, most penny stocks do not qualify. This is because they lack a track record and do not have to meet the minimum listing standards that are normally dictated by the exchanges. It means less information as well as pressure on the company's side and less security for the investor. You will absolutely have to take all this into consideration when planning to invest in penny stocks, as the risk needs to be well worth the reward when you consider investing.

Smaller companies also tend to lack liquidity or at least struggle with it. This means that finding the price within the market and value is far more difficult than with a larger business. Smaller companies are also at a higher risk of being wiped out by a bigger company with their competition, especially if they do not manage to stay up-to-date. Most microcap companies are new, which means they have almost no track records to yet prove themselves to the world and to investors. Some of these businesses might not even have assets, proper revenues, or worse yet, an operation. The low volume of trades latched on top of penny stock trading may make it more difficult for you to sell your shares when the time comes. Because of the low volume trade, it can have a huge impact on the price of the stock. And keep in mind that microcap stocks are a little more susceptible to manipulation or fraud than the larger forms of stocks, merely because they are cheaper to buy and easier to hide the truth.

However, there are still ways and methods of potentially profiting from penny stocks, regardless of whether they are losing value or gaining them. It just means you will have to adapt and change your strategy accordingly to what you believe the stock direction will head toward. This will be explained in depth later in the book.

Penny Stock Tiers

What are tiers in stocks? This is something normally called a "tier market," when investors play favoritism over certain securities that are held within a marketplace. This will result in a higher price for this specific stock group in comparison to others and can sometimes have quite a significant difference.

There are many reasons why this can occur. For example, a group may see a higher potential for higher returns for a specific group, or they may just be exploiting better marketing tactics.

In this modern day and age, any price that fall between one dollar and ten dollars is still seen as quite risky and perhaps even speculative forms of investment. These stocks can drop 50% in value overnight just because of the news or even gain a 100% upward trend if things happen to go well. Therefore, anyone who considers investing in these stocks (normally taking part in day trading) needs to understand that there is always the possibility of incurring a total loss.

However, suppose you do want to put your money into this form of stock. In that case, you will want to have a higher level of security so that you won't necessarily lose the money overnight, and this is where you look at different penny stock tiers.

Tier 1 penny stocks are the ones that you'll want to focus on if you can. This is because they qualify to be listed on exchanges such as NYSE or even NASDAQ. These will be explained in the following chapters. They normally have prices that extend below five dollars a share, but they might even be priced a little higher, considering they are probably more advanced penny stock markets than when they first originally started. Any stocks that fall into this category are still speculative but certainly a whole lot less open to manipulation and fraud, as they do fulfill the higher-level requirements that exchanges ask for. To put it simply, they have a higher capital, a certain number of shareholders, and better financial information has also been provided.

Tier 2 penny stocks are the traditional forms of penny stocks and can literally be priced between one cent and ninety-nine cents. They do not go below one cent, but certain stocks can even be traded at a fraction of a penny, thanks to the digital financial world now available. It is not even uncommon to see stocks that are priced just below a dollar listed on NASDAQ or the NYSE.

However, these companies normally receive a letter, which they usually publicize to the public, that they do need to meet listing requirements (i.e., have their stocks value above one dollar) over a certain amount of time. If they manage it, their stocks will remain listed on the exchange, but if they don't, they will be removed from the list and must move over to the OTC market exchange.

It is critical for stocks to trade above one dollar, as this means that the value never changes to below one cent. However, any stocks that trade below one dollar can even trade down to fractions of a penny.

Tier 3 penny stocks are normally called sub-penny stocks because they are normally below one cent a share. This is where they are merely fractions of a penny and quite low in value. They cannot qualify for NYSE or NASDAQ, which is a massive reason why you should not consider trading with them. They are far from noteworthy and have a low potential, basically an excessively high risk. Losses are more likely to occur with penny stocks that fall under this tier, and you will have to consider your motives if you are interested in investing in stocks that have such low value. Basically, they are not even strong enough to be priced at one cent. This should be proof of the disaster that is likely to await in this company.

Tier 4 penny stocks are when the value of penny stocks is well below a penny (basically $0.0001-0.0009). They are known as trip zero stocks, where they are priced below three zeros.

These stocks can be easily used as vehicles for manipulation. It won't take much to move the market in a different direction. Any purchase can move the stock up by 100%, and this benefits the people who originally purchased the stock. Remember that people will promote this tier, but they are the ones that have stocks in bulk. Meaning any purchases you make, these people will largely benefit from them.

In the end, you will want to focus on penny stocks in tier 1, especially as a beginner, as you are still learning about the markets. When you are more comfortable, it is up to you to invest in tiers below 1, but remember they are a higher risk, and even with experience, it is easy to fall into some of the common traps. It is not always possible to figure out whether a penny stock is legit before it is too late.

However, on average, most professionals try to work with companies that fall under tier one. Therefore, don't hop onto the belief that you are missing out on the impulses of others. Rather, you can consider yourself to be missing out on the common losses and mistakes of others.

Chapter 2:
Are Penny Stocks Worth the Investment?

If an investment is high risk and extra work needs to be done in order to make good investment choices, you may consider whether penny stocks are worth the investments. Extra risk can make things quite daunting, especially if you are just a beginner.

Indeed, the best way to assess that is to look at the advantages. Understand both the risks and benefits, then you can decide whether the risk is worth the reward.

Looking at both the pros and cons can help make you more unbiased when you make trade decisions and can allow you to deal or be better prepared for disappointments or losses if the risks, unfortunately, fall through. The risks are not an absolute guarantee, but every trader can tell you that they have suffered their fair share of losses when it comes to trading. This is all part of the reality when you take on trading. It will never be smooth sailing. The markets are far too random for that to ever be the reality.

Advantages of Penny Stocks

First, you do not need a big account to start. Considering the low prices of a share, it is a good place to begin when you are possibly low on funds. This means you can break the stereotypes and start early on your investment journey, and one of the wisest choices you can make is to start investing as soon as possible. Time is your biggest ally when it comes to investments.

Diligent work and research will get rewarded. If you learn how to conquer the matters of research and discovery of information on penny stocks, then the rest of your investment journey will be infinitely easier. Researching and doing your due diligence is a key tactic to investing, and it is also the difference between an ignorant investor and a savvy one. In all the books, websites, and even podcasts on investments, there is not likely to be a time where people tell you not to do your own research. Trusting others' information or say so, especially on social media, is a terrible choice, but seeing your efforts rewarded can certainly be listed as an advantage as well.

You can see a potential profit on its way up or down a lot faster than common stocks. With penny stocks, you can profit from them whenever they go up or down. Using a short selling strategy, you can still earn an income despite the possibility that a penny stock value may fail. Short selling is the exact opposite of a normal and traditional stock investment.

There is also the advantage of the potential of gains, as penny stocks are smaller businesses, but they do have the possibility of growing. Seeing small investments grow into larger gains is a great advantage for someone who is starting out in investment. After all, profits is one of the biggest motivating factors for investing. Considering there are higher risks, the promises of higher rewards can motivate one to consider investing. That is if you are more of a risk-taker, considering that there is still the lingering chance that things may go wrong. This advantage is pegged with a critical piece of advice: *Don't invest in what you cannot lose.* This piece of advice will act as a cushion if something does go terribly wrong.

Although it might be difficult to track the research, it is certainly not impossible to track the speed as prices rise or fall. In fact, one will be able to see the changes in price within a matter of days. This is also better for someone who is hands-on with investments. Day-trading is a common strategy when it comes to penny stock investments, so this reality makes day trading a whole lot easier and practical. The only factor is that you will need to learn how to track the patterns occurring in the rising and falling of prices.

Because of the smaller prices, it is easier to buy a variety of stocks. When you add diversity to your portfolio, you spread the risks and significantly boost your chances of success. This can also be accomplished specifically for shorter-term investments. Oftentimes, with larger traders that are changed at a rapid pace, the odds of being able to afford a wide variety is slim. This is easily done when it comes to penny stocks. It can also have a generally positive effect on your portfolio. Most of the time, financial experts consider a person's long-term investments, but they are also aware of the importance of a widely diversified portfolio. Having penny stocks also boosts the chances of increasing your liquidity and mixing up the variety of stocks you have. This certainly strengthens your portfolio. Any factors that can boost your portfolio can wrap up quite an advantage, and it is possible to profit entirely from penny stock investing. Although diversification is recommended, there is a great capability to have diversity in a penny stock and to profit from it. Granted, you play the cards right, and you deal with losses swiftly as well as build up some good wins over time.

Exposure is also quite a good benefit, specifically, exposure to other companies, considering that many large companies happen to buy penny stocks. This is already a good indication because not only can you make connections, but the fact that companies invest in penny stocks is a sign of the potential that lies within. Anyone who has worked in the business world knows that exposure is always good. Having an awareness of other businesses and building connections, especially if you are a part of the business world yourself for your regular day job, can help you create an overall awareness of the financial markets. This is a massive benefit over the fact that you can be a step ahead as a norm with enough practice and work. What you learn from penny stocks, you can also benefit from it in normal investments. Although it is different, penny stock trading teaches you about having grit and having the ability to do thorough research with little resources. You might find normal stocks even easier after taking on penny stocks. That is also quite an advantage.

Disadvantages of Penny Stock

In order to make fair, unbiased, and wise choices, a person will need to look into the drawbacks. This is especially important to help prepare you and combat any of the disadvantages should they occur. Having the ability to boost the advantages and minimize the dangers with counter-tactics is a surefire way to help build your success.

Being aware of the risk can also help you to avoid it. After all, while traversing in a jungle to find the treasure, the more knowledge you have of the danger, the better off you are. Learning to avoid as much of the risk as you can is vital to successful penny stock trading, and learning to take the blow when losses do occur is even better; it is pretty much learning how to take a punch in the financial world. Unfortunately, not many people have what it takes to handle a financial punch.

Most of the companies that have penny stocks happen to be of lower quality. This means that the reputation and sales might not grow much further or could easily fail under too much pressure. Therefore, research must be done about the quality of the company, as well as its plans. If it doesn't manage to adapt or take the brunt of competition, then that is a major red flag. In addition, companies that are also swimming in debt is also definitely considered as a major red flag.

As much as people do not want to hear this, most investors will end up losing some money. This is because they are dabbling in risky markets where regulations are practically non-existent. This allows companies to play by different rules, and oftentimes, can lead to more negative outcomes. It is impossible to leave penny stock trading without some form of loss. You must be prepared for this and be easy on yourself when a loss does take place.

Although it is not completely without regulations, it does mean it plays by different rules. If you want to invest in penny stocks, you will have to learn all the different stockbroker regulations for penny stocks. This is important to keep in mind, as you will not be able to practice the same forms of investments, strategies, or rules in penny stocks as you would do for the average stock. Playing by a different rule book means having a better ability to adapt and think outside of the box. If you want things to be simpler, then consider going for the long-term bigger investments.

There is also a lower trading volume, and penny stocks are traded thinly. This does mean that the number of trades that occur is more or less than the average stocks, which means you must play your cards well. Alongside this comes high volatility, which increases the risk of losing out if you are not careful, but that does not mean volatility in penny stock traders is altogether bad. It may mean there is a higher risk, but later, you will learn the positive aspects of the volatility that you can use to profit from.

Next, this is a risk amongst all stocks and shares in the financial world, but because of penny stock's nature, they can certainly be more prevalent for scams. With the lack of information as well as decreased regulations, it is easier to set up a scam, and you must always be on the lookout for this. Common schemes found on the market are pump and dump (where stock promoters rapidly add support for the stock, including by adding huge investments on their own and marketing the raised price on social media. Then once the price reaches an inflated level, they sell their stocks, and investors have literally lost about all their money.

Another common problem that comes with trading penny stocks is the commission fees tagged alongside it. Be aware that most brokerages have a fair commission rate, but penny stocks are an unfortunate exception. Penny stocks have a much higher commission charge, and you should most certainly check out the fees before signing up for anything. It would be a shame for whatever profits you happen to make to be taken by fees, or worse yet, for you to run at a loss. Commission fees are unfortunately a part of working with a middleman and can hinder your progress when working with cheap shares. Again, be sure that you are using the correct exchange and be updated on the commission fees. Do not move and share trades that can rack up too many commission fees; rather, consider your choices more carefully, and keep track of the fees. They will build up over time and can work as a huge disadvantage if you are not vigilant.

However, this isn't the only picture you should see of penny trading. There is a lot more to the game than what you can see through a rifle scope, but this gives you a great idea to make a balanced, unbiased decision. There is always more than one side to a story, and the same can certainly be said for penny stocks investments. A lot of these risks can be avoided, or if faced, not be allowed to hit too hard. It can also give a clear revelation on whether you are cut out for penny stock trading because day trading and penny stock trading are most certainly not for everyone. Make sure you are motivated and make sure you are up for the task because it is a big one.

There are many stories of the success of people dabbling in penny stocks. Although the risks are quite large, so are the options of reward. Looking up their stories, however, you will see they are filled with hard work, mistakes, dedication, and great knowledge of the market they are working in. Unfortunately, good money does not come easily, and that is just one sad reality that makes most people give up within the investment world.

All this may lead you to ask the question: *Can I honestly make a good amount of money from selling and buying penny stocks?* Unfortunately, it can never be completely guaranteed for you, as no one has the full ability to predict the market (otherwise, you would see people being far more successful).

Trading is not that difficult, but many people do not learn the proper skills they need in order to succeed. Many of the disadvantages listed can, in fact, be avoided through the proper research and time spent to combat them. So, to answer your question, if you do not know or learn how penny stocks work, then you cannot build a foundation strong enough to make yourself successful.

Basically, you can earn money. You have the potential to. But hard work, discipline, and tactics can certainly boost your chances. Of course, trial and error are bound to occur, but that is certainly a guarantee in the world of trading. Everyone makes mistakes here, and those who learn from them are so much wiser.

Penny stock trading is certainly not for anyone who wants it easy; it's for people who want to learn. It is quite a process and has a lot to take into consideration. If you want to stand out from the rest, you need to put in the extra effort. What is worse is that it truly is not so hard to stand out from the majority, purely because the majority do not want to take that time and effort. So, basically, this is a recommendation for you to take the time and effort to stand apart from the rest.

Chapter 3:
The Psychology of a Successful Penny Stock Trader

The biggest battle that occurs is not in the investment field but rather the mindset of a trader. Therefore, it is best to have a look at the mentality behind a successful stock trader as well as the top quality and skills in which a reader should develop to improve their chances of creating a profit. The battle of the mind is a great one, and so it is truly best to be prepared. The mind and emotions are all that make people human. They certainly play a role in every decision you make. But in a gaming platform of trading that works on pure and cold logic, it is best to remove certain elements of emotion if you can for your own benefit.

Trading Psychology Explained

As much as people would love to admit that they do not get emotionally involved when it comes to investing, we all know this is a lie. Specific emotions do have an impact on the decisions, which may defy logic and cause a lot of money to be lost. People have gone to war for money, fought for it, and died for it, so making claims that money has no mental effect on you is not only a lie but is completely impractical.

Alongside normal strategies, it is best to tackle the trading psychology that can vastly improve your success. The two most common emotions that come to play in the world of trading are both greed and fear, but there are many other complex emotions that can sway your thinking. However, to start off with the foundational art of trading psychology, it is time to look at the two most guilty emotions that have the largest impact on your overall decisions.

Greed is considered as the excessive desire to gain wealth and can certainly cloud a person's rational thinking from time to time. It can mean taking unnecessary risks or falling into scams because their marketing was a good way to take away the logic to discern fact from false. Sometimes it is good to take a risk, but it can also be dangerous.

Greed can also cause investors to stay longer in the game than they should in order to squeeze out the most profits. You can see this element taking place in bull markets, where investors throw caution to the wind and speculation runs around like a mad hatter. So greed is not altogether a bad thing, as it can certainly make you work for profit, but it can easily go too far, and this is where you will have to learn the balance.

Fear is the complete opposite, as the thought of risks or possibilities can cause an investor to pull out of the game too quickly. The fear of large losses can cause investors to act far too irrationally, causing panic selling and a major loss of profits as well. Fear is normally never a good emotion to feel when it comes to trading but happens to be amongst the most common emotions felt. Fear often leads to other emotions such as anger, anxiety, and even depression, which are all emotions that are detrimental to your overall health and trading choices.

Therefore, both emotions are certainly not ideal for anyone. However, one emotion that tags alongside both is regret. This issue can add to impulsive decisions after mistakes have already been made, which adds salt to the wound.

Importance of Knowing Trading Psychology

Training yourself in trading psychology can help you reduce any forms of error in judgment that could be made, specifically those that are driven by emotions and reactions. This is recommended, especially as a beginner, where everything can certainly feel a lot like a rollercoaster. Preparing yourself beforehand is critical to help you not get overwhelmed. Is it possible to think like an artificially intelligent robot? No, you should expect many of these emotions to arise, but how you handle them is all part of whether you win or lose in the trading world. In fact, one of the biggest losses is most likely caused by choices based on someone's emotions. To avoid unnecessary risk, take extra time and patience to master your emotions.

Mastering your emotions means having the ability to detect patterns and strategies without being biased towards any particular investment and understanding when to hold, despite fears, and when to sell. It is a matter of managing your emotions. This avoids a common no-hold and hope mentality you may find amongst many investors.

No-hold and hope are when you are overstaying your welcome in a bad trade that is occurring. It is holding onto the hope of better trades even if it is unlikely to happen. This is quite a common mistake that is so easily avoidable if only you did not get emotionally involved. This normally involves an investor creating a strategic plan but then failing to keep to it in hope that holding onto the investment will pan out in the end despite signs showing drastically the opposite. Learning how to manage your emotions in order to avoid this is critical for your overall success.

Your ability to manage risk will also vastly improve. As you remove emotional factors, you can replace them with logic and facts, as this is the game you must play in the investor's world. You may make choices to stay or pull out when it is far more practical than if you were to run on greed or fear. It makes a lot of sense when it is mentioned, but when it comes to real-life application, it is infinitely harder.

Personality Types in Trading

First, you need to identify what your personality type is when it comes to trading. Each person approaches investments with a different attitude, and identifying yours will help you overcome any weakness that comes alongside this former personality. There are two primary examples:

Firstly, there is a rigid trader. This is a person who tends to follow patterns they detect as well as rules. They also tend to follow plans to a T. Although this can be helpful for anyone who has a good plan, if the plan were to backfire, it could easily work against this personality type. They can easily struggle with emotions such as greed and fear; greed in sticking to the plan even if it is not feasible under the belief everything will work out or fear that adapting can somehow ruin the entirety of the plan.

Secondly, there is the flexible trader. This trader is far more adaptive to changes, making edits to their plan in the middle of a trade. Although this can also be an admirable quality for a volatile trade, this trader is at risk of changing plans too quickly or veering off course into a great loss. However, the emotion of fear does tend to be more prominent with this personality trait. A willingness to adapt plans under the slightest change can cause issues.

Tips to Improving Trading Psychology

What exactly can you do to improve your mental approach to trading? Well, you must get yourself into the correct mindset, specifically, the right trading mindset. You must remind yourself constantly that stock prices are not personal. They work purely on statistics, numbers, and logic alone. There are no feelings of consideration for the investors, just numbers, and this is what you must remind yourself. This is a battle of strategy and logic, not fear or greed. Do not give trades a personality or life, which may sound strange, but it is entirely possible when you invest a lot of time and effort into doing research. A trade, especially in penny stocks, will always be short-and-sweet and should be approached as such.

Patience is key. Any wise investor will tell you this. Having the ability to wait, or stop yourself before making an impulsive decision, is a great idea. Not only can this stop you from falling into some of the most common scams in investments, but it can boost your success at a rapid rate. Patience allows you to take a deep breath and step away from emotions that may be overpowering you at this point and time. It is giving your mind a break before making any decisions, and it is giving yourself proper time to think things through. Oftentimes, the most common trick scammers use is a sense of urgency and impatience, so already having the patience is slipping the hooks of one of the common investor scams.

Education not only improves your strategies but also affects trading psychology. The more knowledge you have on both the mental battles and the physical battles of investing, the better off you are. How else would you identify investors falling into "fear of missing out" unless you know about it? It is like anger: the best way to gain control of your anger is to realize you are angry. The same can be said for education and investments. The more you know, the better you are at dealing with it on an emotional level. People also stress about what they do not know, or they are afraid. Getting to know as much as you can about trading is certainly one of the greatest solutions you can use to tackle the emotional reactions to trading.

Next is to prepare your mind for the best and worst scenarios. As the one saying goes, "Hope for the best and prepare for the worst." This way, you can have the joy of succeeding and the cushion in case you lose. Imagine yourself winning in the trade, and this can certainly motivate you to work harder. But leave space to imagine yourself losing, allowing yourself to prepare for the worst and disarming that nasty element of surprise if things don't pan out for you. It is terrible to have to recommend this, but the shock factor will not have such a significant effect on you if you practice this technique. It may seem simple, but few people mentally approach a trade this way, as many people prefer not to focus on all the possible negative aspects.

Furthermore, you may find yourself disillusioned when looking at the numbers on the screen. You must keep reminding yourself that you are working with real money here. This allows you to practice more caution in your decisions and more caution if you tend to be more of a risky person. Obviously, if you struggle with fear, you do need to focus on the fact that money is just that: money. Remove the emotional connections you may have with it.

Study Habits of Successful Traders

Apart from trading psychology, there are studying habits, which are tricks people use to improve their knowledge. Keep in mind that everyone has their own methods of studying, so choose your specific style and go with it. Whether it is finding a quiet place in your house, or being among people in a cafeteria, do whatever floats your boat. There is also the common study term known as VARK: visual, auditory, reading, and kinesthetic, where you learn by seeing, hearing, reading, touching, or a combination of them all. It is best to discover the optimal ways you learn to save you a lot of time and effort.

Then the next step is to practice, whether that is working out strategies and trying them out on simulators or studying the terminology. Practice makes perfect and is certainly very necessary when starting out with investments as with any other money-making strategy. As much as one could wish for an easy money-making method, anything worth your time will not be easy. But it doesn't mean it's impossible; you just need some time and effort to practice, discover, and learn. Better yet, find yourself a trader to follow and learn from if you can. Watching their strategies and understanding the decisions they make can certainly help you build your own methods and practices.

Observe the progress you have over time when it comes to your trading. Assess what has improved and look back to the prior strategies you made. Analyze them and be critical. What worked? What did not work? Where can you improve? Where have you already improved? In order to learn from your prior mistakes, it is best to consider keeping a trading journal. It might take more time and effort, but keeping records of your journey can certainly help you identify what you did wrong and what you did right. Focus on asking yourself the 5 W's and 1 H questions: where, what, why, when, which, and how. An example would be: *What went wrong? When did the trade go south? Why did it go south? How can I prevent this in the future? Which trader/news/source caused the trade to suddenly change direction? Where should I focus on improving my trade?*

Staying Focused After Losses

Perhaps the most critical time to practice good trading psychology is when facing losses, as that is bound to happen for anyone who becomes an active trader. Be aware that just because you suffer a loss doesn't mean you are automatically kicked out of the game. It depends on how well you reacted to the loss and how well you spread your losses as well. But a loss is loss, and a person who trades cannot escape the inevitable reality that this will happen sometimes.

However, when facing a loss, it is best not to wallow too deeply. Consider this merely a learning curve and stick with the trading plan you have at hand unless you identify a critical flaw. But it is best to focus on something physical and logical at a time when emotions can be running rampant. Rather than letting loose of any strategy, cling to it just a little tighter.

Keep an eye on market trends, as this can help identify any losses that may occur in the future and help you pull out before it is too late. Remember to place stop orders on your trade where automatic orders are triggered when the stock you have happens to reach a specific price, and place a mental stop in your mind. In other words, pull out and take a break if you need to. This does not mean you have to fully stop, but if a loss is truly heavy, it is sometimes better to take a step back rather than fall into panic and fear and make heavier losses than initially drawing out for a little while in the first place. It is much like taking a step back and an extra-long breath when getting mad at someone—same idea. Allowing yourself to breathe after a long bout of stress and loss is the perfect idea for someone who is just beginning in trading.

But that does not mean your journey ends here. Carry on with the idea that you are still learning. In trading, you will always be learning. Whether it is about the latest trends, technology, or software programs, the world is ever-evolving. And so the world of investing, even in penny stocks, is also changing. Therefore, it is best to stay disciplined in this aspect.

Emotions That Could Ruin Day Trading

If you are participating in day trading, you need to be aware of the most common emotions that could kill your success. It is best to tackle them one by one and be aware of them as you start. Working to build up your resilience and strength against them will certainly help your journey. They are:

- Boredom. Rather than wasting any time, use the free moments you must learn more about day trading. But if you do happen to get distracted due to boredom, you will start taking some unnecessary risks that aren't worth it in the long haul. It is basically taking a gamble, and we all know day trading isn't a casino, so don't take that risk. Learn to avoid boredom by taking certain times off, travel, and even go watch YouTube videos to have a more fun learning experience. There are some incredible teachers out there dedicated to teaching the craft in a way that doesn't inspire you to take a nap. YouTube is a great place for this. Watching motivational videos are also a great way to keep yourself on track and committed to doing the work you need to do.

- Depression. This is a far more serious challenge you may have to face and something that is sadly common amongst traders and investors. Taking losses is not easy for anyone, and some have gone too far when it comes to handling these negative emotions. Many traders can even get depressed after making a large loss or a couple of smaller losses. Therefore, it is wise to approach the financial market with a lot more knowledge and understanding of the risks before even taking a step into trading. Knowledge can help prepare you for both joy and disappointment. Furthermore, only open a trade if you know you are comfortable losing. If you are not willing to even consider the thought of a loss, then it may be time to reconsider whether you are cut out to be a trader. Whether you need some more time and advice, don't allow yourself to be emotionally hindered at a bad trade. Everyone has their bad days, but their success lies in the factor of how they react to them. This is the most common difference between people who fail and people who succeed. It is not how they respond through the good times, but how they respond through the difficult ones.

- Doubt. When numbers and odds flip so quickly, even the most experienced trader may go through bouts of doubt every so now and then. It is a good idea not to second guess every single choice you make. If you walk into trading with an open mind and are willing to learn without dwelling, it can certainly help to reduce a lot of the doubt you may experience. Doubt is a dangerous emotion because it is a close relative to fear. Doubt can cause you to make wrong mistakes just as easily as fear can, so it is best never to regret any decisions you have made, even if they were the wrong ones. The only time you are ever allowed to doubt yourself is when you guessed the total calories of that chocolate bar from a week ago. But steer clear of doubting in a trade; it will only cause more trouble than it is worth.

- Fear. A person could say this is the most popular emotion you will find running rampant in the marketplace. There is even a common concept called "fear of missing out" (FOMO) that refers to you buying an asset against all logic simply because the price is rising or falling, and people are jumping onto the same purchases as well. Fear plays alongside peer pressure, and you tend to see fear at its strongest when it comes to cryptocurrency, a market far more volatile than even penny stocks. Another fear is the one where you are scared to even enter a market. This means you do all your analysis and never find yourself fully satisfied stepping into a trade, no matter what the potential. This means you probably miss out on a lot of major opportunities and profits within the market system.

- Anger. This normally occurs when your doubts and fears come true. This is the time you should take a step back and a deep breath, as there is normally nothing you can do about it now. There is no use stressing about matters that are now beyond your control. The best thing you can do is learn from your mistake, even writing it down in a trading journal, and walk away. This is far wiser than trading in anger, as it can throw all rationality and logic out of the window. This is commonly called "revenge trading," where you try to make up for the losses you have made by taking even riskier trades. And in most of those trades, you are far more likely to make a loss than if you were calm.

- Anxiety. This tends to be a recovery period after a terrible trade. The next few trades you make will probably be filled with anxiety. Remember to relax! It is best to avoid anxiety; otherwise, you can pull out too early in the trade or fail to come up with a good strategy. If you are anxious, then consider starting small with your trades again until you build up sufficient confidence in your skills again. Anxiety again is a close relative of fear, so it normally gets triggered with that emotion. If you struggle with anxiety beyond the trading arena, then it is best to learn how to deal with it in all aspects as far as you can muster. Not only will this improve your overall mental life, but also the skills and decisions you make on a trade.

All of these are quite dangerous emotions. You should consider speaking to a professional if need be in order to help deal with them. Some are easily changed, but others, such as depression or anger, may need some help. You must be honest with yourself, and making wise decisions will certainly help your success in the investing world.

One emotion, greed, though it can be bad for you, can also help grow your penny stock price, but it is certainly bad for succeeding at trading. On the other hand, your motivation to earn profits can help you overlook some daunting risks that many others won't even consider taking on. But this is why it is best to have a healthy balance, both of motivation to earn money but also a healthy amount of fear of risks. That way, you can take risks but pull out of the game if it does happen to get a little too dangerous.

Therefore, it is so important for you to set clear goals. There is no black and white trading to operate investments and trades. If there was, everyone would certainly be successful in trading. Rather, it is like treading uncertain waters. Finding the balance and control of your emotions takes time, practice, and experience.

Mental Tricks That Separate You from Being A Potential Winner to A Definite Loser

There are certainly a lot of mental steps and tricks to learn in trading psychology, so what separates you from those who constantly have pitfalls and mental traps they are not altogether aware of? Here are some things you need to look out for in order to stand out from the average investor.

Firstly, avoid analysis paralysis. When you first start off in the trading world, you will have to soak in a lot of new information. The information tends to come in all forms, shapes, and sizes, including some from your own personal background. Using this information, you will start your practices in the world market. Your first trade can certainly be quite scary despite everything that you know. Hopefully, your first trade goes smoothly, and the money comes rolling in. However, if you are unlucky, then you will start to understand why so many traders tend to give up or fail. This is called facing loss, and your first loss can and will certainly hurt.

The trick here is to get beyond the despair, hurt, or disbelief that tends to crouch at your door as a trader. So how exactly do you do this? Well, consider that you just spent a couple of hours or even weeks crafting an amazing trading strategy. But when you test it out, only one of six trades world. Any savvy trader will know that patience and setting up a large enough sample of the traders will truly reveal how effective the strategy is. But someone who is a beginner may get paralyzed and pull out of the game due to doubt and fear (the common emotions) before even seeing the true potential of the strategy they took to develop. This can quickly lead to getting disheartened, as nothing seems to work, which forces people to quit before they are even properly in the game.

It is best to accept that the market is random. By understanding this factor, you will have a better mentality that can lead to profits. You can spend all the time in the world working on predicting the markets, allowing you to feel a sense of control, but sometimes, even so, predictions fail, and so do analyses. Accepting that this is how the market works can allow you to release a lot of the frustration that builds up when you try and predict the markets. It's just not worth that stress. Predicting is good; despairing over a failed prediction isn't.

Here is some bad news. It only takes one trader to invalidate the analysis you have made, especially when it comes to penny stock investments, where trades can so easily get influenced. Now it doesn't mean you will necessarily fail over an invalidated analysis, but it does mean that you should not place all of your trust on it. It can only take one person to help grow or decrease the value of the stock, depending on how much they evidently invest in or remove. So again, it is best to remove any emotional attachment you have for the market and do not take it personally if it does not head in the direction you thought it would. Otherwise, you may see your profits cut a lot shorter or even at a loss because you followed your analysis with utmost dedication.

Shutting out the noise is another good mentality to take on. What exactly is the noise? This occurs when you have too much information from too many sources about trading, specifically drowning out your own thoughts, strategies, and ideas. Basically, signing up for newspapers, spam emails, and feeds giving off the latest tips and tricks will only confuse you more. The best way to drown out the noise is to do the research on trading when you want to and to occasionally ignore what people may send you. A lot of these newsletters, emails, and updates will contradict each other because they are based on a variety of different people's opinions, so it is certainly best to develop your own and move on. Sure, it is great to learn from others, but to get flooded with the next tip or trend without you actively seeking it out can cause a lot of confusion, which will cloud your path.

It is easy to say you understand there is a risk. Anyone does that when climbing on a rollercoaster or eating a piece of bad chicken without much thought of the consequences. But thinking things through and grasping the understanding of what the risk will cost you is important. You may say that you are willing to take on the risk of the trades (inwardly, as you still do not want to lose the money—who does?), but this will only be reflected when you happen to suffer a loss. This can trigger a lot of dangerous emotions mentioned before, especially if you were not truly ready for the loss, so we cannot stress enough how important it is to accept the randomness of the market. However, again, this is only going to work if you can afford to lose the money. If you cannot, then naturally, you are going to be emotionally invested no matter what. Therefore, do not invest what you cannot afford to lose.

Learning when to take the profits is another mental trick that can help you with penny stock trading. It sounds easy enough, except that many traders get hooked with the possibility of what could happen next. This is a similar mentality of a gamble, where many people continue to place bets after having a few wins just out of the pure thrill and possibility of earning more. A good trader knows when to pull out of the game despite what promising opportunities may lie ahead, as this avoids taking on unnecessary losses again. Figuring out the times to walk away will be doing yourself a massive favor.

Finally, realizing and admitting when you are wrong is another great tactic when it comes to stock trading. This may sound strange, but an unwillingness to admit defeat or mistakes from time to time can do you a massive disservice. On the other hand, when you admit that you are wrong, you are also acknowledging a willingness to learn from it. When you learn to accept these factors, it can save you a lot of time and money, which will allow you to move on.

You need to develop a winning attitude. What exactly does this mean? It means you get into a mental place when you approach the market with a can-do attitude. You should fully accept what the market throws at you, but also what the market is willing to provide, reducing the unrealistic expectations that tend to take place left, right, and center amongst a lot of people. This does mean not allowing doubt or fear to get in the way. There is nothing wrong with acknowledging risk and dealing with it if it does come true, but doubt and fear can easily pull away from the winning attitude you need in order to stand out.

Winning at a trade has very little to do with the system you use, the equipment, and internet speed. It all comes down to the responsibility you take with the results and acceptance of what you receive from the market. It may not always be positive, but having the endurance and grit to push things through will get you further than merely training in facts and knowledge. This is as much of a mental battle as it is a physical one, and this is something you will have to accept.

Keep training yourself mentally. As much as this is a battle of strategy, it is also a mental battle. Those who are aware of this factor tend to have higher rates of success. This is because they can play on the emotional waves of others while steering clear of their own. Understanding the behavior of common investors will help you identify a lot of the volatility that goes in penny stock marketing, as well as help you diffuse a scam. It also keeps you away from making irrational choices, so we cannot stress enough how important the battle of the mind is with penny stock marketing.

Remember to stay on the positive side. As much as a trader's life can sink into pessimism, allow your eternal optimist to flourish just a little regardless of whether bad things happen. The ability to see the bright side even in a bad trade can get you far.

Chapter 4:
The Basics of Investing in Penny Stocks

The first step to building a house is the foundation, and so the same could be said for learning or building in any category. Learning the basics of penny stock investing is about knowing the foundation, which is one of the most critical components of building towards your success. Next, of course, you want to build up for yourself an empire of trading experience and hopeful profits. But you must start somewhere, right? Sometimes shaving everything down to the basics is what you need exactly to benefit from making the right trading decisions.

How The Stock Market Works

Stock markets do carry a certain element of risk with them, but one thing that has been proven time and again is that if a disciplined approach is taken with a stock market, then it is certainly one of the best methods to build a person's net worth.

Stock markets can be considered a common marketplace where people can buy and sell shares in companies. Stocks themselves happen to represent the ownership of a company, and the prices are set depending on the supply and demand in the market. It also can be called equity or share. Therefore, the value of a share depends on the level of activity that derives from both buyers and sellers. Stocks also act as a form of representation to have a certain amount of claim on its assets (what the business specifically happens to own), as well as some of its earnings.

Companies often want to raise capital larger than a bank loan would allow. Furthermore, they do not want the burden of having to repay a bank with high-interest ratings. This is a common reason why they issue shares in order to increase scalability without creating excessive debt. Raising capital is a great way to boost the growth of the business and profits, but sometimes businesses do need large amounts of money to start. Capital growth is the primary reason why companies issue shares. In order to grow at a faster pace, you do need to raise funding in a fast and efficient way.

There are two main forms of stock: common and preferred. The main difference that does occur between the two normally involves voting rights. Common shareholders hold the right to have a certain say and vote in the meetings, such as when the board of directors or even auditors are voted upon. Preferred shares do not have such voting rights, but they do receive a higher preference than those in common shares and are more likely to receive dividends or assets if the business were to liquidate.

Stock Exchange

The stock exchange works like a second-hand store in real life. This is the platform where existing owners of the shares can sell them to potential buyers. Buyers do not interact directly with the companies on this platform but rather with the shareholders themselves. This emphasizes the reality that public companies normally don't have as much control over who purchases their shares.

Listing Shares

When a company is first launched, it will need a large amount of capital and can get it from operations such as a bank loan, but then again, why get into debt when you can sell your shares to the public? This is normally done through an initial public offering (IPO) and can change the status on which the company officially stands. Normally, the IPO offers early investors the option to cash out and the ability to reap handsome rewards, which is all well said and done if the business is successful.

Once the company's shares are indeed listed on a stock exchange, this is when the shares can fluctuate as both traders and investors alike work on assessing the value.

How Share Prices Are Set

The most common area where the price of a share tends to be set is in the auction process. This is where buyers and sellers place bids and offers to buy or sell the shares. The bid is the price that the buyers place and the amount they are willing to pay, whereas the offer is the amount the person is willing to sell for. The supply and demand determine the average price for which shares are commonly sold for.

There are many different forms of ratios or metrics that can be used in order to value the stock, but the most common formula is the Price-Earnings or even (PE) ratio. This is a great way to figure out more about the analytics side when it comes to the financial world of the company.

Returns on Stock Investments

Returns on stock investments, otherwise known as ROIs, work by figuring out the profit or loss made with a specific investment. A person can normally do this by subtracting the final investment amount from the original cost you had invested. Evidently, if your answer happens to be positive, you have made a profit. But if the answer is in the negative, then you have suffered a loss. You can also calculate the number of dividends you have received, as this will add to your profits.

Stocks are normally classified in two ways. One is known as market capitalization, which is the total market of the company's shares. The other is by sector, where the stocks are classified by the Global Industry Classification Standard. The Global Industry Classification Standard is the industry taxonomy that was created and launched in 1999 by the MSCI as well as Standard & Poor. This was used for the global community of finances.

Where Penny Stocks Trade

Now you may like to know what direct sources to look for. Below are some of the top listed marketplaces. What you do need to understand is that each brings its own unique advantages to the table, but they also have downfalls, as there is no perfect system after all. It is best for you to decide what works for you and what risks you are indeed willing to put up with. Some of the exchanges listed are not even recommended, but rather here to create an awareness of what you should consider avoiding as a beginner and even as an experienced trader.

NASDAQ Small Cap Market

NASDAQ Capital Market, which was known until the year 2005 as NASDAQ Small Cap Market, has a primary list of small-cap stocks, but the name changed to reflect a big shift in focus. Companies listed here have the desire to raise their capital. It means that small businesses did not have such a burden to be listed on this marketplace and could also grow through the NASDAQ listing.

The advantages are that you can invest after-hours extended trading hours, in comparison to the NYSE that can only manage trading with the open hours of the day. After hours with NASDAQ means you can trade up to 8 p.m. in the evening at times.

There is also online automation using this platform, where you can trade from the comfort of your own home. Having the ability to access this platform online removes the need to administer trades on behalf of the investor. Rather, the investor can take a lot of the trading responsibility into their own hands. However, this does allow a certain level of higher liquidity and more control over the choices you want to make.

However, keep in mind that Nasdaq does not carry the same level of prestige, and many of the listings are known to be quite volatile. Furthermore, keep in mind that penny stocks bring disadvantages of their own.

OTC-BB

OTB-BB stands for over-the-counter bulletin board, in which you secure trades via a broker-dealer network. This moves away from the centralized exchange centers and can involve equities, debt instruments, and other forms of derivatives. Taking away the middleman is always an advantage for people who prefer to stay anonymous, and you can find a lot of the equities that are not listed on the current exchanges. These equities are normally called over-the-counter equity securities.

Greater care needs to be practiced when working on the OTC marketplace, as the security and regulations are indeed far looser. This means that scams are quite common, as well as businesses that frequently fail.

Amex

Amex is an iconic and global financial brand that has racked up billions of dollars in revenue and has thousands of employees across the globe. It is popular and quite advanced in years.

Amex is a relatively solid choice considering its long history but never an absolute guarantee. There is still a consistent growth in revenue and taking strides to remain competitive against other growing markets. It is also starting to take on a more digital focus.

However, there has been a slight fall in the results of the year's earnings, and this can be quite concerning for investors, as Amex is a little behind in the competition. In addition, it is facing a lot of challenges as a card provider, and the dividend returns are also quite small in using this platform. These are all things to take into consideration.

Canadian Markets

The Canadian stock markets have been doing remarkably well and are rich in resources, as well as having quite a sound financial sector. As safe as the economy and situation appear, it is best to approach them with an unbiased viewpoint.

Firstly, the Canadian currency is strong, and trades are going well so far in Canada. As mentioned before, Canada's banking system is incredibly sound. There are plenty of resources, especially in companies and stock exchanges. This makes it incredibly tempting to invest in penny stocks in this sector.

But be aware: there is a lack of diversification, which means that there are many sectors in this industry that are sorely lacking. Moreover, it is still a small market, so even if you were to consider investing, it might be best to diversify your portfolio in other markets as well. There is also a currency risk despite it being strong. If inflation levels rapidly start to rise, there will be a lot of heat on the economy as well as on Canadian banks.

Pink Sheets Penny Stocks—Steer Clear!

This is mentioned here only for the reality that it is not recommended at all. Pink sheet stocks have been considered good investments, as they work as a quotation service and not an exchange for trading OTC. However, here comes the big problem: pink sheet stocks are thinly traded and lack a lot of liquidity. Many of the companies using pink sheet penny stocks are quite worthless. To put it plainly, it is just not worth the risk to invest with pink sheets penny stocks, as you are far more likely to suffer a loss than making a gain on this platform.

Penny Stocks Straight from the Companies

Investing directly with the company removes the safety of regulations that are still in place despite being penny stocks. There is absolutely no guarantee of a fair valuation, and you are far more likely to get scammed or ripped off. There are too many companies that are scraping by the edge of their teeth and the investments coming in from ignorant bystanders hoping to get some return. The odds are too small, and you have no proper protection from the investment you made.

Penny Stocks Over the Phone

This is just a bad idea. Firstly, you can never properly verify who you are talking to on the phone, and secondly, it is likely to be a scam. A person should not have to explain why trading penny stocks over the phone should *never* be considered.

Buying Penny Stocks: Basic Elements

There are some basic elements you will need to know and check up on when buying penny stocks. In order to proceed, you will need the following details to complete your order:

Firstly, the ticker system. This is the name of the company, which you will probably need to know. You will then need to know the market on which the penny stocks are trading. Considering you want to target a specific company, it is best to know where to work on the exchanges after all.

You will also need to decide on the number of penny stocks you want to buy. This is typically considered the volume of shares and the amount you have in your budget. For example, if you have $2000, and the company sells shares at $0.50, then you will want to order about 4000 shares if you are buying all of them at $0.50.

You will also want to set a market or limit price. This is for trade orders or shares that you are not completely sure of the price. In order to make sure the trade price will go through, it is best to limit the price. For example, by setting it at $0.70 per share, you will not pay any more for those shares. Therefore, if they are selling it at a ridiculously high price, you avoid getting ripped off from the company.

You can also decide on the duration of your order. Normally, market orders do not require a form of duration, but if you are willing to wait for your share to reach the ideal price, then you can have your order fulfilled when it hits the trading floor.

Limit orders, on the other hand, need a duration, and you will also get an additional limit order duration.

Next, you will want to figure out the total cost. It is best to consider not just the price of the shares but also the commission costs and any other fees that may come alongside it. Again, having a budget and estimation of the prices can help prevent any nasty surprises from coming your way.

Then you will need an open order. This is the duration before your order expires, and it is certainly considered to be open. It is best to keep an eye on your open orders, which should be easy to check if you have an online brokerage account. It is a great way to check and see the shares you have purchased and the price you have paid for them.

Selling penny stocks involves the same elements as buying stocks, just in a matter of slight reversal.

Instead of paying for them, you are obviously selling them.

Picking A Stockbroker

Considering they are the middleman, picking your stockbroker is quite important, and there are two types of stockbrokers you need to be aware of. They differ in a few areas and depending on your goals, you will want to choose different stockbrokers.

The first is the discount broker. Naturally, you pay a smaller fee for them, but it normally means they simply follow your orders. You will have to do your own research, and any decision you make will reflect nothing on them.

The second is the full-service broker. You pay a higher fee for them, but they will spend more time giving advice, direction, and drawing up a portfolio plan for you. This is certainly more suited for clients who are invested in larger portfolios and thus are willing to pay higher commission fees.

Broker Criteria

How do you decide on the right broker for you? There are several steps you can take for this. Firstly, you will have to determine your own requirements. It does depend on your situation and circumstances. It is also ideal to have one broker instead of three or more, no matter what the temptation may be to add variety.

You will have to check out commission fees and make sure it is affordable for you and that the speed at which the broker works for order execution is to your liking. You will evidently want a broker that is reliable and understands the policies of penny stocks, as not every broker may know how to deal with them.

You will need to check out the broker's accessibility if issues should arise, as well as the level of customer service. If customer service is difficult, then it will be a massive pain to work with them.

Furthermore, it is best to check out a customer's research and their available tools. How well are they able to stay up to date with the trends, and what tools do they have available? Being up to date is important, but that does not mean all brokers adopt this policy.

Candlestick

Another tool to add to your kit is the candlestick, which is a type of price chart used for technical analysis. It displays both the high, low, open, and closing prices of the security for a specific period. They tend to show investors whether the closing price of a market was lower or higher than what the opening price was, which is critical to understanding how the stock market is truly faring. Thus, it is excellent for traders who are specifically looking for chart patterns that may occur.

The reason why it is called a candlestick is because of its candlestick appearance on the market itself. The name originally came from Japanese rice merchants and other traders who were far ahead in recording financial management before it became popularized in America.

The top of the candlestick represents the highest price of the day, whereas the end of the candlestick represents the lowest price of the day. The thicker centerpiece at the top represents the opening and closing price, and so does the thicker piece at the bottom. The body of the candlestick is either black or red if the stock closes at a lower price, but it is white or green if it closes at a higher price.

The shadow of the candlestick represents the day's high and low moments, especially in comparison to how a stock market opens or closes.

Ultimately, the candlestick represents the impact of the investor on security prices and is more than often used for technical analyses, as it is directly linked to the company in the financial aspect of its stocks. This is a handy tool to use as a penny stock investor, and you should learn all about it before even setting your foot into investing. Candlesticks are used for any technique when it comes to trading many forms of financial assets, such as stocks or even foreign exchanges.

When a candlestick is white or green, it is normally a sign that there is a lot of buying pressure building upon a particular stock. This tends to be an indicator that a certain stock is "bullish." But it is important to look at the candlestick within the context of the overall market, as it can give a good indication as to why you should or should not consider investing in it after all. When you see a lot of red/green candlesticks, that is an indicator that there is overall a lot of selling pressure and an indication that a market is in a "bearish" state. What does it mean when a market is in a "bearish" or "bullish" state?

A bull market is when a stock is starting to rise and trade on a more continuous basis. This is normally an ideal scenario to get caught up in as a trader, especially if you are focusing on the long strategy.

A bearish market indicates a drop in the prices, where a lot of people want to sell the stock. And believe it or not, a person can also benefit from this through short selling. But this form of profiting is far riskier and will require a lot more experience in order to be able to pull off something such as that.

Now coming back to the candlestick: Traders can take advantage of candlestick charts to effectively analyze literally any cycle of trading that occurs at any point and time in the day. You can even use it to analyze a minute of trading or up to an hour. That is all up to you to use at your discretion and wisdom. In short, there is a lot you can learn when it comes to candle charts, and their usefulness will not be diminishing any time soon.

Two-Day Candlestick Pattern

These are more based on short-term strategies from the information given on candlestick patterns. These trading patterns normally signal a reversal in trends, where the first candlestick has a short body and the second towers over the first. This is normally called a "bullish engulfing pattern," and is good to keep an eye out for. The "harami" is the name called for the complete reversal of this trade, where the first candle completely towers over the first.

Three-Day Candlestick Pattern

This is commonly called an "evening star," where it starts with a bearish pattern and quickly turns into an uptrend. The second candle shoots upwards but has a narrower body, which is an indicator for less volume. The third candlestick, though, tends to come at the middle part of the first candlestick. The reversal, called a "morning star," is a more bullish pattern.

It is important to make sure you completely understand what is going on with a candle chart. Take your time studying them before investing, even practicing out these tools or techniques mentioned via paper trading first before putting any real money into it. However, a candlestick chart pattern is advantageous to know and is probably one of the major tools that traders use to help win their success.

Chapter 5:
The Trader's Toolbox

Every person needs a toolkit for their practice. Being a trader is no exception to this rule. To become a penny stock investor, you will need a tool kit to refine your craft and trade penny stocks effectively. In summary, it is boosting your chances for success.

http://finance.yahoo.com

One of the easiest tools to use is websites such as http://finance.yahoo.com. It is one of the simplest, free tools to use to check on the percentage of gainers. Sometimes, however, considering this is a free tool, it may mean that the figures are not always as accurate, as less time and effort is spent on their accuracy.

http://www.stockopedia.com

This is another great free tool for you to use. It gives simplified charts and other forms of information for you to use in your journey as a trader. There is also a paid version available, so if you like the free version enough, then you can consider taking on the paid one, especially if you would like to know about all the financial credentials of a certain amount of stock.

http://freestockcharts.com

This is a platform that is run by the Worden brothers

and is known to be the backbone of TC-200 200 software. It is extremely useful for technical analysis, and you can even get greater detail if you pay for the premium version. Again, this all depends on your budget, but it is great to consider tools that can just make your life easier when it comes to manners of research and analysis of the specific stock. It will make your journey more successful, as you will be able to spot more dangers as well as opportunities.

http://stockcharts/com

Much like the tool above, it is a great charting tool, and again, has greater details in the premium version, as to be expected as the developers would like to make some money from the equipment theory they are creating.

http://www.sec.gov

This is a great platform to keep a watch out for and search for sec filings that you know you are looking for. To top it off, this is a reliable site, so you will likely find what you are looking for here. Nothing is more destructive to a person's success than unreliable information, so it is always best to double-check any tools and sources you are using for your trading.

http://stocktwits.com

This is a website that gets ideas when trading different types of stocks.But be careful who you believe when using this site and don't ever trade with someone else's trading idea unless you fully understand their strategy and have the same conclusion for yourself. It is great to draw ideas from those who have been in the game longer, but ultimately, it is your money that you are risking. Therefore, it is best that you definitely stay responsible for any plans that you undertake.

http://www.microcapsearch.com

This is a cool tool that is useful if you would like quick access to other websites that provide information about stock and important data. Basically, it is a great research tool that helps to provide you with the information you need.

http://candlesticker.com

This is a great free tool that you can work out the candlestick patterns you have learned in the chapters before. Evidently, this is a great source to analyze the overall success of a certain company's opening and closing stock.

Some of the most common tools you will need for penny stock investing, and should certainly be something to add to your toolkit, include:

Stock screeners. These can scan the entire market and give information on the average trading volume that is taking place, chart patterns, etc.

Charting software. This shows the performance of a stock, fund, or index over time.

Stock simulators. Ideal especially for beginners, this is a platform you can use to practice fundamental analysis or even test out trading strategies without having to necessarily spend the money. You can also work on the simulations during your actual trading process, especially to test out new strategies that you may have developed or the ideas of others, to see how it works out. Keep in mind that the simulation removes the emotional element and doesn't manage to take all the costs.

Trading newsletters. These are email or print messages that normally inform traders of unusual market movements, new developments, and innovations. Keeping up-to-date is critical in the investment world, especially when predicting the overall success that may occur. It also provides expert opinions on how stocks will hopefully move in the future and what stocks have the most potential. Now, extra work may need to be acquired to find the experts' opinions on penny stocks.

Criteria for Evaluating Stock Research Tools

- Finviz stock screener
- Moomoo
- Stock Rover
- Yewno | Edge
- Motley Fool Stock Advisor
- Benzinga Pro
- MacroRisk Analytics
- https://www.benzinga.com/money/stock-research-tools/

Best Brokers for Penny Stock Trading Links

- <u>Fidelity</u> - $0 per trade
- <u>TD Ameritrade</u> - $6.95 per OTCBB trade
- <u>Charles Schwab</u> - $0 per trade
- <u>TradeStation</u> - $0 per trade
- <u>Interactive Brokers</u> - $.0035 per share

Chapter 6:
Building Your Strategy

So how exactly do you go about making a strategy? This is a good question and certainly deserves a detailed answer. Research is the first ingredient to a good trade; the next would be a well-thought-out plan. As the saying goes, failing to plan is planning to fail. A strategy is a detailed and logical plan, after all, and it is best to understand the steps you can take as a beginner to formulate one that can hopefully get you a good profit.

Before You Start

Before you start with real-life trading, it is best to practice paper trading. There are a few steps you can undertake here when practicing, as you do need a few steps and rules when starting off. Besides, it is an easy as well as a realistic method for you to learn the ins and outs of trading without having to spend a dime. In all honesty, there is no disadvantage to a paper trade that can weigh down the advantages that a simulation truly brings to the table. Especially considering it can help prepare you and wrinkle out many mistakes without having suffered major losses like many people who directly start with trading certainly will suffer.

When you start your paper trade, it is best to both choose as well as write or type (if that is more your thing) your objectives. You are not just trading and risking your money to have fun; you have goals. And in order to remember and stick to them within a specific time frame, it requires you to write them down and remember them. The biggest lie you can tell anyone is that you do not need to write them down because you will remember them, which is highly doubtful. Furthermore, if you are not clear of the path you want to take, jotting down where you would like to go and what you would like to accomplish can truly narrow the path for you and give you a better idea of your objectives. Setting down the objectives for penny stock trading will make a huge difference, so don't hesitate to bring that pen and notepad with you, or even a tablet. Whatever floats your boat!

Then you will need to choose your favorite forms or types of penny stocks. It is best to have familiarized yourself with the markets you want to trade upon and choose a niche you are interested in and motivated to work in. It is wise to know the price range of the shares and the industry groups you do enjoy. Remember to set any other parameter you may have found to be important when looking up those specific penny stock markets.

Then you should decide the steps you will take when it comes to research, monitoring, and the trading of shares. It will certainly be quite exciting when you start off, but you need to know where you will begin.

Which websites do you trust? Will you directly call the company? What reports do you intend to read through? Do you understand all the information that is available? Would you rather get professional help and opinions? What information sources will provide you with the best details that you need at the end of the day?

The next step would certainly be deciding on a broker unless you already have one. This is evident once you are confident with the paper trading, and all the practice you have is now ready to take the next big step. Be sure to pick a good and reliable stockbroker that is tailored to your specific needs.

There you go! Seven steps and ideas you can follow when you start with penny stocks. Not so complicated after all, but it will take a good amount of time and effort to put together. But once you get the ball rolling, things should certainly be moving at a much faster pace.

Once you are ready to start finding penny stocks to trade, here are a few things you need to consider doing:

First, research the company. This is a no-brainer, as being an informed trader means you are a smart trader. The best way to start this off is by doing a quick Google search, but this will most certainly not provide you all the answers you need. It can help you filter through the worst of the stocks, though, and determine whether the stock in question is worth spending more time on to research.

Do pay attention to the news tabs on Google search, as this is a commonly ignored feature but important and likely even useful when it comes to researching stocks. Considering there are more informative news articles than blog posts regarding the stock in question.

You will then want to look at the volatility in question. When it comes to penny stocks, it may seem ironic, but you are not looking for non-volatile stocks. Instead, you want to work with stocks that are spiking at quite a rapid pace. These are the stocks that normally have the most activity, and therefore the most promise to gain a profit (but also a loss). In these modern times, you will have more than enough software to be able to help filter the penny stocks that you are looking for. If you struggle to understand why, think of it this way: the less volatility that occurs in a trade, the fewer buyers and sellers there are when it comes to penny stocks. This means you may have quite a lot of trouble with selling your shares and overall liquidity.

Volatility in penny stocks is good and can push you way ahead of the curve when it comes to penny stock investing.

The next item you want to look for is the volume that is in the trade. Volatility is not the only factor that can determine whether a stock is a good choice or not, but it does help. No matter how promising a company appears to be, if it does not have a lot of volumes, then do not consider even trading it.

Trading volumes that run under 200,000 shares a day is pushing it, and if you want to play it safe, go with stocks that trade under 500,000 shares a day. High-volume is a sign of a large amount of interest that exists in the stocks. That means if you decide to sell, you will not have many struggles to find a buyer and that the level of liquidity that exists in that company will not or should not be difficult.

Next, you will want to look at the catalysts. Catalysts normally act as a predictor of a major event that is occurring, specifically news that can have or move a stock price regardless of whether it would be a good or bad move.

For example, if a company is about to release a brand new and exciting project, you will find it on the catalyst and possibly predict for it to have a positive impact on the company, if the product is successful, that is.

Whenever you are considering a stock, it is best to take a sneak peek at the catalyst and watch how exactly they are making the stocks move. You may even build a better idea of what to watch out for and get the hang of the trends that impact stocks.

It is good to hear the opinions of others. It does not mean you should always listen to their advice but understanding the thoughts and perspective of others can help you give that extra edge. This advice does come with a warning: it is a good idea to check what people say about penny stocks, even on social media, but always take it with a grain of salt. This should merely be a form of research and should not have any sway on your ultimate and final decision unless proven by other facts and actual reliable sources. However, at the end of the day, it is truly best to learn to think for yourself. This starts off by observing the actions of others and deducting yourself whether their moves are accurate. You aren't merely copying what they are doing but learning how to apply certain circumstances in your own favor while discarding the choices of others that will not work in your scenario.

History also has a knack for repeating itself, but never exactly to the letter, much like experiencing déjà vu. However, learning the patterns of penny stocks can give you a relatively good idea about how certain penny stocks may work out. It might be recommended to trade based on the same key patterns that occur time and again. It may seem a little boring, but it is quite reliable. And as a beginner, you need to consider applying this strategy until you get comfortable with other forms of strategies or simply stick with it if it works. That is entirely up to you.

When it comes to trading, you need to consider the time of day. In a busy life, it is quite possible to lose track of time. But when it comes to trading, it is important to keep track of what is happening. And if you have another job, it is best to adopt a trading schedule that works around yours. If you are a student, for example, then you can study and attend classes in the mornings and focus on trading in the afternoon, or even vice versa if it suits your schedule better.

The time of day you happen to work on trading can certainly change the strategy you want to take on. For instance, certain stocks are great for working on during the morning but can come up at a total loss when the day closes. This is where picking up patterns can come in handy to adapt them to your time and availability.

Avoid companies that have massive loads of debt. Any company that is in debt is a massive red flag waving from a high tower. So when you check out a penny stock company, it is important to understand all the aspects of the business, and this most definitely includes the overall financial health of a company.

To determine this, it is best to rely on the technical form of analysis but keep in account the fundamental accounts too. Take your time to read the reports to have a proper grasp of what is happening inside of the company. This is normally a good indicator of the company's health, and if you see the business is drowning in debt, it is not likely to be successful. Does this mean you cannot trade? Well, you can, but you would have to adjust the strategy and keep in mind that the debts will play a massive factor on the stocks. As a result, you are at a higher risk of running at a loss.

You would want to keep an eye out for penny stocks that do have higher and more favorable ratios in their liquidity. Every company has its fair share of assets and debts, and when you compare the two, this will reveal the liquidity ratio. If the company has a higher ratio in assets than debt, then it is more ideal because it is a key indicator that the capital of the business outweighs the debt. This means the company is functioning quite well at this point in time and holds promise for action in the future.

Next, you will need to consider using a stock screener, as this will help to narrow down the choices you make based on the criteria you have set down. In addition, it can allow you to search a larger number of factors, volume, volatility, etc.

Tips to Develop A Penny Stock Strategy

First, you need to have a healthy respect for the risk involved. This is likely to develop over time, but don't ever ignore it. Don't fear it either though, just have respect for it. Wherever you can, work on avoiding the risk. It is just overall better in the long run.

Be clear on the goals you have. Be crystal clear because the better idea you have about what you want, the easier it is to come up with a concise plan.

As a beginner, it is recommended to start small. No matter how keen you may be or what you have indeed learned, starting small and building your way up reduces a lot of risk and cushions your losses when they do come from time to time. Furthermore, starting small, especially at the beginning, curbs any massive problems or debt by completely avoiding them in the first place.

Another great tip to shorten your learning curve is by choosing a mentor. You specifically would want a mentor who has indeed walked the same path as you hope to. The mentor can help by preventing many of the mistakes you could make and hiding you too different strategies you may not have considered. Again, it is wise to learn to think for yourself, but no one said that you weren't allowed any form of help after all.

Do not take an extra risk by forcing a trade just because you feel like a trade should happen. If you need to force a trade, it means you are doing something wrong or perhaps a little hastily. Rather, wait for the trade to come to you, and do not make any decisions about a trade that thoroughly diverges from your original trading plan without a solid and verified reason.

Things to Look For in Stocks While Day Trading

When you are working with penny stocks, it is known to be more of a hands-on approach. This means that you are going to have to learn the craft of day trading in order to take advantage of the more volatile market that runs throughout the day.

Here are some things to keep an eye out for when you start off and progress in day trading as a penny stock trader. These are tips to find the potentially hottest trade that runs on that day:

First, it is a catalyst. News happens to be one of the primary causes of stocks to move upwards or downwards at a rapid pace. That is why it is so important to stay updated on the trends and news without having that bias, but if you can predict a trend, then you can also find yourself ahead of the curve, which is the ideal scenario.

You also want to keep an eye out for a low float stock. This is where insiders and actual major investors do tend to have ownership of most of the shares. This means there is a limited number of stocks, and the shareholders are quite limited to selling. This ultimately means that the demand and supply work well, and a lot of price fluctuations will be occurring there.

It is obviously ideal if you can spot a killer chart pattern. This is when you discover a pattern that has a promising trend to use for your benefit. Therefore, it is so incredibly important to learn chart patterns, as your day trading will benefit from your understanding of patterns and chart readings.

Evidently, you also want to look for signs of the increased trading volume. This is when you see a rise in shares being traded over quite a short period of time. This is normally a big indicator of hype over a specific stock and trader piling in to get their load of some good profits.

Key Terms to Know as a Beginner

Trading has its own language, and it is important to know what people are talking about. However, you will discover that learning the language yourself is not too complicated, and here are a few terms you do need to be aware of as you kickstart your day trading:

Long: Long stock normally means you usually own stock where you earn money if the price rises and lose money if the price lowers.

Short: This occurs when you borrow a stock and sell it on the market. You are then under a certain obligation to purchase the stock back and even go on returning it. You profit with the vice versa strategy, where you earn a profit if the price falls and come up at a loss if the price rises.

NYSE: New York Stock Exchange, which happens to be one of the largest exchanges in the world. Multiple of the world's largest companies are traded on this platform, and therefore NYSE is a massive and popular platform for traders on a global scale.

Support: The support level that appears on a chart is when a clear level of market or security happens to drop in its history. For example, if a certain stock reached seven dollars and they bounced down several times, then seven dollars would be the official support level.

Resistance: The exact opposite to the support level, where a level at a specific market has dropped in the past before bouncing back up. If a stock declines and stops at seven dollars before rising again, then seven dollars would be the official resistance level of the penny stock you are investigating.

The Official Step-By-Step Guide on How to Trade Penny Stocks

When you are reading about a penny stock, you are under a higher risk than the actual trade. The risk is multiplied when you add pink sheets and OTC exchanges instead of the traditional NYSE and NASDAQ exchanges.

That is why it is crucial to have strict and serious criteria under which the penny stock will fall, and it is why you want to practice matters such as risk management.

One idea is that you can focus on day trading penny stock. As you may have seen mentioned time and again, penny stocks are far more suited for the short-term game, and normal stocks are certainly suited better for the last.

Another popular step for risk management in trading is not to hold your stocks overnight, where the most the same can be done without you knowing.

Now the first step you can take with day trading is by trading only the best and simply leaving the rest behind. It is a simple concept that falls under the idea that you must have strict criteria. You can use a stock scanner, which can make your life so much easier for you and cut a lot of the work time you have on figuring out trades in half, if not more.

Each morning, you can start off by listing the stocks that fit under the criteria in which you will trade.

The second step is to trade the best quality setups. The first step is trading with the best stocks. Now, you want to be able to trade with the best setups, such as bull flags or even flat top breakout patterns.

These are the chart patterns most professional traders simply trade, considering they are at the lowest level of risk, and they also share many similar characteristics. They normally both require stocks to make some big moves up, then a quick pullback that happens to have a sell-off. If you ever find yourself in doubt, consider asking and finding out whether the stock you are selling has a once-a-year type of event that occurs. This is normally the ideal time to jump in and trade with this stock. Normally you can identify a bull flag when you see the candlestick on the sales of trade, making a new high right after the pullback has indeed occurred.

The next step is to join a community of traders in a chat room if possible. In order to be one of the best traders, it is certainly helpful to surround yourself with the best. There is a lot you will be able to learn from them, as well as a supportive community that can help you with your trades, problems, and even mental tricks. Don't follow a trader's advice blindly, but as a beginner, you are certainly allow yourself to learn more from people who have practiced the art of trading for years. Although, be sure that the chat room you join for traders has professionals, and be aware of scammers as online communities are famous for misbranding. However, a big positive benefit is the likelihood of having a community that informs others of a trade that shows great potential. The likelihood of a good trade getting spotted is infinitely higher and can be a great advantage as well. Not only do you learn from them, but a community's knowledge and like-minded goals can have you reaping profits you may have never reached on your own.

At the end of the day, you may find the repetitive patterns to be quite boring, but sometimes repetition is necessary. There is not a massive secret ingredient or recipe to becoming a multimillionaire in trading. But learning from the best, following what works, and sticking to the rules can certainly pay off in the long run.

Chapter 7:
Research & Analyze: Tips and Tricks

You certainly would have heard time and again that the key to trading is research. There is no doubt that knowledge is power and is critical when it comes to the decisions you need to make. But how exactly do you do research on a topic that has little information? Where do you need to look, and why do you need to look for this info? There are certain steps you will need to take in order to gain more confidence in analyzing penny stocks and ensure they are getting the best returns.

How to Get Information About Microcap/Penny Stock Companies?

This is a tricky question, as one of the disadvantages is the level of difficulty to retrieve information on the penny stock. However, just because it may be difficult does not mean it is altogether impossible, and there are certainly a few things you could do in order to get the information you need. Keep in mind that if you struggle with information or nothing pans out about a certain penny stock, then you do need to steer clear. The less information that is shared, the more likely it could be a scam. Transparency is certainly a thing to be desired when searching for a good company to invest in.

Firstly, it is best to ask the company whether it is indeed registered with the SEC and if it files the necessary reports to the SEC. Suppose a company is small enough not to have to comply with this. In that case, you can also consider calling your state regulators in order to get the information you need, as well as the company management and brokers who have recommended for you to invest in the company. If you already know anyone who has invested in the company, ask them how it has been faring. But remember to be cautious and wise with the information you receive. You need to consider whether the management has the proper experience to execute the business plan it advertises. This means you should have a good knowledge of how a business should be run. This may seem obvious, but most people do not have that piece of common knowledge. You may need to consider whether the company also has the proper resources or any form of competitive advantage that show any good signs of succeeding. Finally, be careful when reviewing the company's website. Even checking out the quality and design of it can certainly be a good indicator of how up-to-date it is with the digital world. You can also contemplate searching for information on the company on the OTC market websites.

You can find information from the SEC, as many companies are required to file their reports with the

SEC. This means you can use the SEC's EDGAR database to discover which company files at the SEC itself (so if you do not get a hold of management, you can always check there), and you can receive the reports that the company has sent in to file. However, if a company does file their reports to the SEC but does not place them on EDGAR, you can reach out to the SEC's online form or email the public information office to find out the information you need.

You can also look up the information at your state securities regulator. This is especially valid if you have difficulty finding the information of the microcap company directly from the company, your broker, or even the SEC. As you can see, you do have a few options and sources to find out the information you would like. When you contact the state securities regulator, you can check to make sure whether the company has been legally cleared and allowed to sell securities in your state. This is a sure-fire way to avoid most of the scams and cons out there, as most traders will not go so far with their effort to discover the information necessary. But laziness comes at a price, and so does knowledge. So take your time to make sure you are confident in the company before bringing any sort of money even close to them.

You can check from other government regulators as well. For example, many companies do not have to file reports to the SEC, such as certain banks. However, the banks or companies do need to have filed updated financial information at their own banking regulators. And many of the regulators are quite easy to access online. Therefore, you can discover what you need in the comfort of your own home.

Another common source of information is reference books, websites, and even commercial databases. It may not be a bad idea to pay a visit to your local public library or the nearest business or law school library. You will find many referencing materials that happen to contain information you may need about companies, especially the company you will be interested in. In addition, you can access commercial databases, which may have far more history about a company's history, products and services, management, revenues, and even go as far as the credit ratings, which is critical to see how a company handles its debt. Again, occasionally doing proper research requires going the extra mile. This is certainly a wise example, but better to get the needed details than regret it with a massive loss later. Considering that the SEC cannot endorse or recommend any form of business, using the commercial database gives room for consultation and possibly a more expert opinion on how the companies are faring. Being unbiased is demanded by law for the SEC, so as a beginner, despite getting the necessary reports, it may be wise to start consulting with professionals in the commercial database.

You can also consider going to the secretary of state, where the company is specifically incorporated.

Contacting the Secretary of State is a good way to find out whether the company is in good standing. It might even be possible for you to receive copies of the incorporating papers as well as annual reports of the company you are indeed interested in. These are all good sources to consider for penny stock companies but do keep in mind that just because companies do have the appearance of readily available information or file reports does not altogether mean it is safe to invest in. Check out the reports and be careful with your investment decision. It is still a possibility that a company is perfectly legal and can still fail, or the company is good at masking its true intentions. Again, this all brings about the element of risk. That is why it is so important to practice caution and why you will be reminded of this repeatedly throughout the course of this book.

How to Pick Penny Stock Winners Pre-Strike

What should be the determining factors for choosing a penny/microcap company? There are certain rules you can follow and keep in mind when it comes to a penny stock.

Look for the stocks that you can see are already spiking. One of the fastest ways of identifying this is by finding a stock that is already moving. This can normally be seen through charts and other forms of analysis. Keep in mind that due to information inefficiencies, it might be difficult to catch it from the beginning, but it does not mean you can't hop along while it is still a part of the move.

Keep an eye out for any potential breakouts that may reach new highs. Looking for a stock that can reach new highs, especially during the day, is a rewarding strategy to be aware of. For example, if you see that it is indeed a Friday afternoon and the stock is still holding the same high as in the morning, there is always the potential for a short squeeze before the market closes. For a penny stock trader, a short squeeze is most definitely something you need to learn to recognize in the marketing world, as it can be rewarding for you in the long run. This is because when potential breakouts do happen to reach the new highs, they will not be able to keep the price in their previous resistance level, and in the end, you will be earning greater profits than even possibly planned.

Another rule of thumb to follow through on is always betting the price on the action. The price action basically gives you a real story about what is happening with the stock. Companies may lie, but numbers and figures don't. You can figure out whether a stock is breaking a new high or starting a downward trend, even if the news sites in the entire world give no indication of what is occurring. The stock charts are an important and relevant tool of information for you to use at your full capacity.

Take your time to watch price movements. If anything, it will be educational, and although it might be quite tiresome, this is the best way to catch on to patterns that you certainly will not have noticed on otherwise. Make it interesting by turning it into a game. Place bets for yourself on which stock price you believe in moving next. If you are wrong, figure out why, and if you are right, feel free to reward yourself with a good cup of coffee or tea. You certainly did earn it!

Once you start gaining more confidence in your betting game, you can consider placing money into your predictions, or if you still don't feel too confident, paper trade and build your way up until you work with actual money. Keep in mind that sometimes, you still are going to bet wrong, but it is best to learn from it and move on.

Next, do your research. This is no surprise to you, but this is one of the most common reasons traders fail. Laziness is a terrible word to use, but unfortunately, it is a reality in many investors' lives. People like to trust what others tell them instead of doing the grunt work themselves. But grunt work does pay off, and in the end, you will see yourself far more rewarded than those who attempted to wing it with the bare minimum of information.

When knowing the best penny stocks you need to buy, consider the following: remember former runners, hot sectors, sympathy plays, and news. They all play a role in penny stocks and should be something you will actively keep tabs on. It may seem like a lot of extra work, but it is entirely necessary to stay sharp and much ahead of the game as needed. Success does require a lot of hard work as well as determination and grit. Success requires you to go over and beyond what most people are not willing to do. It may not be fun, but it is necessary.

Consider this: If you are willing to take just another half hour on learning all that you can about penny stocks as well as the company, then you are way more informed than the majority of traders. That gives you leverage and an edge that most other people don't have.

Another aspect is to think like a retired trader. You only make a move if you must. You are not going into retirement, but thinking in this mindset can help you maneuver against the pent-up emotional plays that tend to string along countless other traders. People who have a "retired" mindset will not come out of retirement for a trade that is barely valuable, if it is worth anything at all. Do not waste your time on so-so traders. You are not shooting for a minor league; you are working for the best trades.

Selecting A Penny Stockbroker

Choosing the right broker for the job is a good tip for success again. The top penny brokers do charge reasonable fees, but they are also quite supportive and tend to be far more friendly. So there are certainly a lot of qualities you will need to consider when choosing a penny stockbroker. But just like choosing penny stock, you will need to do the same amount of research on a stockbroker to make sure you know what they offer and whether you can sufficiently trust them.

Consider whether the stockbroker has an online or even possible mobile trading platform. Determine whether you could have access to the online or even mobile version of a broker's app. Using this method, you can know whether a trade is going against you or for you wherever you are.

It is also best to check out the minimum deposit. Although many online brokers do not require this, it is always best to completely make sure. You will obviously want to have a fund regardless of the deposit fee or not.

Supply & Demand and Tape Reading

So, where do supply and demand come into play with stocks, and what on earth does tape reading mean? Well, a tape can be considered as a brief summary of all the trades that had occurred during the day. It shows people the price, size, and time of the trade made individually. It is a good strategy many penny-stock traders use to analyze the movers that occur throughout the day as well as seeing and identifying the fluctuations and potential opportunities that occur.

When a trade is executed, it is normally called a print, which is the total number of shares that had been both bought and sold. It is the price at which the share had indeed been sold, as well as the time at which the trade happened to take place.

For most trades, they occur at the asking price, which happens to be in green color. If the trade does, however, occur at a bid price, it will be in red, and if the trade happens literally between the two, then a person can see it in white. This might not mean anything of too much importance, but it is good not to make any false assumptions about the information and specifically its color codes, as red is normally understood in a negative light, especially in the financial world.

One of the ways you can use this to your advantage is by picking up the specific patterns of the trade that is occurring. For example, you can pick up the speed at which the shares are moving, as well as the volume and the offers and bids that are being held.

Short Sale Restrictions (SSR)

This is a short-selling strategy you can consider but is not normally recommended. However, it is always good to know how it works. For example, if the stock happens to decline at 10% or even more from the close of the previous day, the SSR will basically be set in motion to restrict the amount of trading occurring with that stock until the end of the next trading day.

This rule does apply to any stock, no matter where they are traded, but this rule can have a massive impact on penny stock traders. Any declines of more than 10% could work as a great advantage in day trading, but this then gets heavily manipulated in the restriction that had been placed a decade ago. It is advised not to practice short selling, but if you are considering it, then please be advised that the restrictions will act as a major disadvantage when trying out this strategy. You may struggle to make a profit with this one.

Technical and Fundamental Analysis

You will have to practice both fundamental and technical analysis when it comes to the specific stocks that you will want to buy. So, for example, although you may not necessarily be looking at penny stocks when it comes to the long term, it doesn't mean they are exempt for the same amount of analysis as you would when it comes to other stocks.

Fundamental analysis occurs when you look at the company itself, specifically its earnings, the economy, and the financials that are happening within the company, as well as keeping an eye on the information that is related to the specific company itself. This is a bigger and more important factor when you are strategizing for the long haul. However, it is still a good practice to be aware of what is going on in the company when taking on penny stocks. You might not have to focus so intensively on the long-term future.

Technical analysis has more to do with the stock charts, the data that is trending, as well as any other technical factors that have to do with the company's financial performance, specifically regarding its shares. This is a critical skill you will have to learn when it comes to trading penny stocks, and important that you understand the full scope before diving into penny stock investing.

Scanning for Stocks to Trade

There are thousands of strategies in the world that you can find and use when you are trading penny stocks, but they will not all work for you and your circumstances, nor the company that you are interested in investing in. Therefore, it is important to practice in a simulation to see what you are comfortable with and, just in general, to help you figure out what exactly you are doing. There are a few rules that you can focus on following to help you out:

First, you can focus on doing some pre-market research. This is where you will find stocks that work with your specific criteria before the market even opens for that specific day.

Second, it is important to look for "gappers," which is when something big is happening in the company, like massive news that has been released. A stock that happens to be gapping is when it fits all good criteria points for trading but is at a lower point than you thought it might be.

Third, you will need to have a good understanding of chart patterns. This is where math in school paid off, as you will now have to learn to read them carefully. Many strategies are reliant on the analysis of the candlestick chart, and it is best to identify when they are having an upward or downward trend.

This is speculative data, and a lot of deductions need to be made. However, if you practice these methods correctly, you can make quite strong and potentially accurate instructions for the long hall. This is especially helpful if you spot items such as a bull flag pattern. This normally defines items such as risk points and is a great indicator of when you need to pull out of a specific trade.

It is important for you to get comfortable with speculation as penny stock trading focuses more on having a good grasp on behavioral aspects and the picking up of patterns.

Avoiding Scams

Apart from common rookie mistakes, scams and fraud are most likely to be one of the most common forms of downfalls that do occur for a trader. However, the likelihood of recovering losses from scams is small, and it is just best to normally avoid them altogether. Here are the top tips to keeping yourself safe and avoiding these scams when it comes to trading:

Firstly, consider every penny stock recommendation as a scam until it is proven otherwise. Next, you need to look for the source of the report and make sure you understand where the information of the business and stocks come from. Recommendations could so easily be made from paid promoters or insiders of a company. Check and double-check!

Secondly, steps have been given for you to properly investigate a company. Consider the rule, "Investigate before investing." This will save you a lot of pain and trouble in the long run. Be careful when you read their financial statements and any other forms of information you may get a hold of. The more information you gather, all the better, as again, the more transparent a company is, the less likely it is to be a scam. After all, legal companies normally have nothing to hide, but scammers have so much to keep in the dark. If you cannot find out enough information about the company, then play it safe and don't invest. You need to have a good amount of confidence to even consider placing your money into an investment.

It is also good to look for the exchange. Finding penny stocks on some of the major exchanges is always a good sign. If you find them on OTC or pink sheets, it means they normally don't meet listing requirements on the major exchanges and are likely to be a higher risk.

If you can, do your best to verify any claims they do make. Those who promote penny stock tend to make lucrative claims such as a potential massive release or a promise of the gold mine or a bucket of gold at the end of the rainbow. Basically, they will lie. That is a fact. It is best to discern which company is telling the truth and which ones are grasping on desperate marketing tactics. Do not fall for the bait as many people do. This will again only get you into massive trouble. Be sure that the companies' claims are backed up by legitimate sources.

Always be skeptical rather than gullible. There is no such thing as a quick-rich scheme. Those who managed to get rich quickly are purely through a stroke of luck, nothing more. Follow the rule: "If it is too good to be true, then it more than likely is." Playing it safe than sorry is generally the better rule of thumb to follow.

If you are investing and trading online, it is also best to take extra precautions when you are working on your computer, tablet, or smartphone. Basically, any device that has an internet connection does happen to be vulnerable to hackers. So when you are working with money online, it is certainly best to ramp up the level of security that runs on your devices. You should definitely consider getting a VPN so that no one can track you or your movements online. This may not seem too important as an investor, but online security is the same as taking your money and valuables to a safe.

Be careful of the messages you receive, especially phone calls. If you receive phone calls from a company out of the blue, then alarm bells already need to be going off, considering that most companies do not call unless they are a scam. Also, double-check any links that are sent to you and be aware of phishing sites that might look almost identical to the original website.

Basically, practice extra caution, and if something seems off to you, then steer further away.

Additional Tips for Research

Avoiding scams, looking up companies, and making sure you are a step ahead are all important tips. There are, however, some additional tips you can follow through on to help improve your overall chances of success as a trader.

You can start off by checking the SEC website for the stock listing status. It is a good idea to know where a company stands with the SEC, regardless of what information you may have garnered directly from the company itself.

You can also focus on getting copies of the company's most recent SEC filings from a fee online financial provider. Again, it means free information that gives you a nudge ahead in the right direction.

You also need to take a step into your business shoes by figuring out how exactly the company is making money and how much it stands to make using the financial report. This is best to determine and verify any claims that they do make, as well as see if they are running as they should. In general, it is a great way to see the raw and truthful potential of a business. It may be time to brush up on a little accounting as you sneak a peek into the financial world of the business you take an interest in investing in.

Finally, you can pick a penny stock that is trending with a minimum volume of 100,000 shares. This is a good rule of thumb when finding good penny stocks.

All in all, there are many tactics and strategies you can find. But at the end of the day, a lot of these matters are based on the decisions regarding your specific circumstances and budget. You need to work out whether the risk is worth the reward, whether the companies pan out, and whether you are following through on a great strategy. Be careful with every choice you make, but if you do make a mistake, learn from it, and don't beat yourself up about it because everyone makes them. Being a savvy investor means you won't give up but rather that you'll try again. It is a game of logic, after all, and though you may have lost in one move, you certainly can plan how to strike on the next.

Chapter 8:
Effective Trading Strategies

You are not alone when forming a strategy. In fact, there are many strategies available for you to use as you kick-start your investing journey. It would be wise to start with them first before developing your own strategies, as this can give a more practical idea about the trading world without having to create a plan from scratch. Building experience is equally important as designing a strategy, as they normally work hand in hand.

Scanning, Searching, And Striking

There are three rules you need to follow with one of the trading strategies. These are good steps to follow, especially as a beginner:

The first step is scanning. You can use a stock scanner to find penny stocks that fit into a certain category; basically, the best penny stocks that have the highest potential for success.

You would want a market cap that falls safely between $50 million and $300 million. You will also want the target price to be 5% above price and the current volume to be above $1 million. It is preferable to target penny stocks in the US and purchase shares that are under $5. On technical matters, it is best to focus on the price to be above $200 a day as a simple moving average.

The second step involves searching. You will have to filter between the results that scans have revealed, looking through the watch list of filtered stocks to find the best pattern. You will want to find the stocks that have the clearest price action. These penny stocks have the highest potential and should be considered seriously after doing the necessary research on the companies, as well as analyzing their success. Do not leave it merely up to a scanner to tell you whether you should invest in this specific group. It only helps you narrow down your options, but it is important to verify whether an investment choice is good because artificial intelligence focuses on statistics, not reason.

Then, once you have found the stock you are interested in, it is certainly time to strike and hold on to the stock until you wait for the pattern to be confirmed.

Trade Penny Stocks That May Interest You

Another option is specifically selecting companies that you are interested in and sticking out for you specifically. Then, do the necessary research, making sure it is extensive, and consider all the external factors. External factors are items such as an economic outlook and geopolitical climates.

Remember to use limit orders. This can certainly help to limit your losses and works when predicting the stock's trends. Limit orders should also help to buy and sell at the prices you can benefit from, with you having to constantly monitor your stocks 24/7.

Tier trading occurs when you split up the initial capital and purchase stocks at different tiers. For example, you can start with a smaller starter position in order to validate the trading thesis. The moment your stock increases, then you add a second tier.

Top Patterns to Know When Penny Stock Trading

Every trader has their own personal traders when they are trading. As a result, Penny stock trading has a lot of technical analysis involved rather than fundamental analysis.

Penny stock technical analysis tends to work with chart patterns as well as indicators. So the best way to learn how to work with them is through paper trading.

Support and Resistance Lines

Support and resistance lines happen to be important for any trader. They point out all the points of strengths and weaknesses a company has undergone. This is vital because it shows traders the best time to enter and leave stocks. Basically, patterns emerge, and identifying them will allow you to increase your chances of profiting, learning when to buy and sell. That is ideal, especially for a volatile platform, where it is best to know when to leave and when to climb onboard.

Support lines are normally drawn when a stock bounces at a specific price—for example, one dollar. If the stock happens to approach one dollar again, traders will start to bounce off and move upward. The same could be said if the stock has a two-dollar resistance line, as this normally means the stock will have an incredibly difficult time breaking the two dollars.

When you use the support and resistance lines in trading, you will need to understand that when the support is broken, it becomes resistance, and when the resistance is broken, it becomes the support.

Bull Flag

This is another common penny stock chart pattern. In this matter, it is important to see the consolidation and continuation. Bull flag patterns only occur when there is generally a strong move upwards and have shaped about 1-3 candles.

Whenever there is a significant movement in price, the volume must be present. If a bull flag does happen to form on little volume, it means that it is difficult for the stock to break out. A breakout only occurs when a seller finally steps in. Basically, it does not have a high rate of liquidity if it struggles with volume.

Double Bottom

This penny stock chart pattern is the reversal of a continuation pattern and can be just as beneficial for investors. The double bottom pattern happens when the price of a stock reaches the same low price twice but then pushes itself back up. This normally gives the chart a "W" shape. It also means the business can recover from losses and has done so before. It is generally ideal for investors to jump into this when the stock is bouncing back from the second low that it has had. But it is important to keep an eye on the stock traders over the next couple of days in order to make sure it is carrying on with its uptrend. Because despite what the pattern may indicate, there is still a level of unpredictability, and it is wise to remain cautious despite what the chart might be revealing.

Golden Cross Chart Pattern

This is known to be quite a lagging indicator, but the golden cross does happen to be one of the most sought-after patterns when it comes to trading. A lagging indicator normally confirms certain trends are taking place and not predicting them. This is because the chart uses a past price action instead of the currency action that is taking place. Normally a golden cross happens to occur when the 50-day happens to be a simple moving average across the 200-day moving average.

This is normally considered to be a bullish sign for a strong upwards trend. Traders normally use this golden cross form if they are in it for more long-term trades. Seasoned traders also use indicators other than the golden cross to fully confirm their decisions when they are buying penny stocks. It is the mark of a savvy investor to always double-check the information given. It would be wise if you adopted the same trend and form of thinking. Never take something at direct face value, even if it happens to be coming from a chart.

Fibonacci Retracement

This is a trading strategy that is quite a bit more complex than those covered before. Normally it should be used in line with other chart patterns such as the bullish flag, a way to confirm or verify a specific trend. This is a good chart to use as a day trader, and you normally draw the chart from the previous day's close to the high of the day.

All these strategies and tools can be considered as a stepping stone and a helping hand when you first start trading. You can even consider using them as an experienced trader if you find levels of success and profits in them. Work on sticking to the plans and rules and be careful not to get emotionally attached. The best way to start, including reading the charts and picking up the patterns, is by using the simulators that are readily available for you to use.

A good strategy is critical for your success and is certainly a carved path for you as a beginner. Keep these strategies in mind, and even discover others on your own. Find out what makes the most logical sense for you. Be entirely sure that you do understand the strategy itself before following through on it. Because if you don't understand a strategy, then how on earth do you expect it to work?

Chapter 9:
Do's and Don'ts of Trading Penny Stocks

When you learn about penny stock trading, you are bound to make a couple of mistakes. But it is certainly better to avoid many of them by learning from the mistakes of others. This is by learning the certain do's and don'ts when you are working with trading penny stocks. First, you need a good understanding of some things you should never do and what you should rather consider doing instead.

Do's in Trading Penny Stocks

A rule every wise investor follows is as follows: only invest with risk money or funds that you can afford to lose. We cannot stress enough the importance of this choice and how people have fallen far by blatantly ignoring this rule. Many people have put all they have in hopes of gaining more, only to lose and struggle to get back on their feet. In short, they became far worse off than when they began, and you must absolutely avoid this. Never put in money you cannot afford to lose. Just do not do that to yourself.

It is best to keep your sights on the decisions and movements of experts in trading. Many of them are

110

quite public with their decisions, educating others with what they have learned. It is best to keep an eye on them, as they are far more likely to pick up problems more efficiently than you could on your own. It does not mean to follow them blindly and question their decisions in order to understand their logic and build your own, but it is certainly a trick to success to learn from the best.

Start paper trading, as this is the simulation that has been mentioned before—a great way to practice your craft without necessarily risking your money. Most expert traders still use paper simulations to test out their new strategies. It just makes sense. If you have a field to practice in, then why not take advantage of it? You will be taking some time and learning in an environment that is far more friendly than real life. Now, it takes that emotional element away, and you can only practice such matters in the real trading world. But it certainly helps you to prepare. And it is no surprise that those who use paper trading have higher chances of being successful than those who jump into it blindly. You are far likely to suffer fewer losses simply by testing out your strategies on a platform that can give you an idea of whether your plans are flawed or practical.

Buy what you know. If you do not understand your market, how on earth are you supposed to pick up when a business is doing well or making a sharp incline for the worst? If you cannot understand whether the business is staying ahead of the competition or merely in one place, then failure is right at your doorstep.

It is best to be passionate about what you are investing in. This can act as a greater motivating factor to do your research, as well as have a greater understanding of the industry. For example, suppose you are interested in cycling. In that case, investing in businesses with cycling trails may be quite practical as you will understand what bikers enjoy and whether the business is running as it should be or has the potential for growth. On the other hand, you will not have the same idea when it comes to a fishing business if you do not take any interest in fishing. If you do not understand a specific business, then you should do enough research and studies on it until you are confident enough before investing. This can save you from making blind decisions.

Remember to set goals. If you have no pathway you want to follow, then again, you will be stumbling around with no good purpose. You need to set for yourself SMART goals and make sure they are practical for your lifestyle and budget. You also need to learn to stick to your goals as far as possible and only change them if absolutely need be or to greatly improve your success after you learn a particular goal may not have been so practical, as that is also a possibility.

Try out different sources for investment picks. Again, this is diversifying your investments, giving a cushion for a business to fail, or gaining success on one business while the other merely trudges along. As a penny stock investor, it is a lot easier to diversify your portfolio as well as the different markets, considering it is far more achievable.

However, pick specific industries to focus on, so although you can have a variety of businesses you are interested in, make sure they all fall into similar niches. This can give you space and room to master the knowledge you need of that niche. Otherwise, you are bringing on yourself a massive headache by picking vastly different industries, and keeping track will inevitably be a nightmare. Again, it is best to focus on a few industries rather than a vast amount.

Remember to call investor relations of each of the companies you choose. It is certainly great to get into contact with the businesses themselves. Even if you do not invest directly with them, it is not recommended. Thus, finding out directly from them the information you would like to know.

Watch and wait. Don't immediately jump into investing. Instead, take time to practice trading simulations and ensure that you are confident with your strategy. Keep an eye on the business you are interested in and keep analyzing it. Considering penny stock movements occur within days, you will not have to wait too long to understand how the business works and which direction it is currently heading in.

Always gauge the outcome of a given trade and learn from what happened. Regardless of whether it had a good and bad outcome, it is best to study and understand what went wrong or right. Being able to identify these steps can certainly help you in the future, especially in avoiding certain mistakes or jumping onto another potentially successful trade.

Remember to cut losses as quickly and as calmly as you can. If things do happen to go downhill, and you can clearly see this, it is best to jump in and cut losses as quickly as you can manage. The last thing you want is to wait things out, only to lose well beyond what you could have saved had you decided to jump in and cut your losses immediately. However, there is a delicate balance when it comes to this, as some people cut their losses too quickly and end up missing out. This is a decision you will purely need to make if the scenario does happen to arise.

Also, do not be afraid to get out of a trade when the performance doesn't match the realistic expectations you have set. If things do go slow, or have a steady decline, then it is best to leave the board again before you lose out.

Take small wins and gains in order to prevent big losses. Sometimes you may not earn as much as you want to, but it is better to win a little less than lose a lot more in the trading world. Some risks are certainly not worth taking.

Remember to be flexible for both long-term and short-term growth. Although it is good to have endurance and stick with a plan, if there arise some unexpected circumstances, adapting your plan to best respond to them is critical. Also, being flexible means staying up-to-date with the latest tools, news, technology, and even trends that tend to spring up left, right, and center within the trading world.

Keep a detailed trading diary. This is perfect for making sure you record both your successes and losses. Being able to back-track and recall your actions in the past is especially important to make sure mistakes won't be repeated and successful strategies will be used again. On the other hand, it is near impossible to remember every action you take or every decision you make. Keeping a journal is especially ideal if you want to review a trade gone wrong or right and you would like to understand the path you took that had brought you to that point.

Take on predictable gains. If it is predictable in trade, why skip out because it is predictable? This is just common sense, after all, and not a battlefield. You will want to take hold of every opportunity that is thrown your way, and if you see quite a predictable gain, don't be ashamed to go for it.

Use scanners.

Be humble and always willing to learn. This is how people succeed. If you listen to the success stories of thousands of people, you will hear many similarities spread throughout them all. Many of them, being humble about how they had gotten this far. Give credit where credit is due, and keep an open mind. This means being willing to learn from others, even if they might have less experience than you. They may have different points of view. Being humble will also allow you to be more careful with the choices you make, allowing you to avoid unnecessary mistakes that normally come at the price of being arrogant.

Be okay with starting out small. Everyone must start somewhere; and again, it is best to keep an open mind about where you can start and what you can afford. In fact, you are being kind to yourself if you approach trading with a realistic mindset and work on growing your capabilities as a trader. Keep in mind that most success stories don't happen overnight, and everyone does have to start somewhere.

Don'ts as A Penny Stock Trader

Do not simply invest in whatever is the "hottest industry." Although it is great to be aware of the trends, sometimes following the route everyone else does is a common mistake. Rather, only invest if you are confident in your plan and strategy, not just based on the speculation of others. Oftentimes, what you see when it comes to the "hottest industry" are people buying out of FOMO, where logic flies out of the window. This is especially the time to practice caution and be aware of the reason why a specific stock is trending. If you cannot see a valid reason, then stay far away because it is far more likely to burst once the illusion of a company's success is discovered.

Do not give any attention to the non-volatile as well as illiquid penny stocks. Non-volatile means they are not moving fast, sure, but it also means you are far less likely to earn something from them in the long haul.

Do not listen to your gut, especially when you are emotional. Investing drains your emotions and brings out panic or greed. Without having the firm boundaries of logic and reason in place, then you are going to fail long before you even come close to succeeding. A lot of people in movies say to follow your gut, and sure, when it comes to certain matters such as people, an emotional feeling is what you need. However, trade does not operate that way as it works on strategy, and therefore it is best to double-check every decision you make to ensure it does not ride on emotion because that is a quick ticket out of the trading business.

Do not believe in press releases or what social media tells you. News has a way of lying or telling half-truths, even when it comes to trade. So why even consider using it as a reliable source? It is best to handle any social media posts and press releases with a grain of salt. Remember, the truth can easily be twisted in any way people want it to be. It is best to discover the truth through sources other than press releases and most definitely other than social media, which can be a thriving base for scammers.

Do not be desperate for a trade. Patience is a virtue in any investor's world. It is certainly far better to wait for the trade to come to you. Although speed and proficiency are necessary for certain elements of trading, waiting is certainly another. You can consider trading to be far more of a marathon than a sprint, where time is your ally and patience is your skill.

Do not expect big gains in the beginning. Especially if you yourself have a limited budget, and you just start out trading. Having a realistic mindset on such matters can save you from a whole lot of disappointment, and you should certainly keep this in mind as a beginner to save you from making radical decisions after suffering your first loss.

Do not be afraid of taking a day off when there are no great plays. Taking a day off can be quite relieving, giving you rest and time to have a new perspective on matters. Trading is stressful, and taking a day off when you see the opportunity is certainly recommended for everyone. Being able to come back the next day refreshed and fighting will set you ahead of your competition who did not take the break.

And you should trade only if you have $50 to even $300. Certainly, any less than that will mean you are likely to suffer a loss from commission fees without getting high enough returns.

Do not buy penny stocks unless they have a great catalyst.

Although it is good to take a day off from trading, it is still best to check in on the markets every day if possible. It might add a little stress but keeping an eye on the updates is critical in fast-moving trades, especially with penny stocks.

Do not ever go all in, despite the promises and potential a penny stock trade may have, because this is not a poker game. You cannot play a bluff in hopes of fooling the market. Remember to weigh on the side of caution and be careful with where you put your resources. Going all-in on a particular stock despite its promises is a foolish move because although you have the possibility of making great gains, the pendulum can switch just as easily over to a great loss. Then you will be kicked out of the game, such as in poker, if your bluff or card loses.

Do not always believe in gurus. Keep in mind that they are making money from teaching webinars, but they will always hold something back. They will certainly not show every single trade they make either. They help others succeed to a certain degree but always keep a missing piece to themselves. It is simply the way it works for them, and you need to keep this in mind. There is always a truth or reality missing from what they may be saying to keep you behind. It is best for you to discover this truth rather yourself rather than relying completely on them. How else do you think they are going to profit from you?

10 Rules for Penny Stock Trading

1. It is best to ignore the penny-stock success stories spread via emails and social media because this may instigate people to copy their steps. The problem is that what may have worked then will probably not work now. It is best not to be influenced too much by success stories that probably did not explain everything about their process either.

2. Don't listen to tips, and do read disclaimers. Penny stocks are sold more times than they are purchased, mostly through the tips that come from newsletters or emails. The newsletters do not give you helpful tips. They are marketing for money purposes in disguise of helping you out, so it is best to ignore the disclaimer at the bottom of the newsletters, as companies are paying them for exposure. But this does mean that many newsletters make a lot of false promises about companies who are far from the quality of the newsletter itself even.

3. Sell quickly. Take any profit you get and move on. Lingering in penny stock trading hasn't done anyone much good except gain loss. Once you have made over 20% to 30% profit, it is a good time to sell. Many traders, however, hope to gain far more, but getting too pumped up is a common mistake a lot of people make.

4. Don't listen to company management. This may sound weird, but in the murky world of penny

stocks, don't always believe what you hear from companies. You should be picky about what you trust, especially companies that are biased towards their own stock. Many penny stocks are scams that work to enrich people from the inside, so it is best to do thorough research with sources that extend well beyond the business itself.

5. Don't sell short. Although short-pumping penny stocks may seem like a good idea, it is too volatile to consider. If you happen to be on the wrong side of the trade, you will be racking up quite a heavy loss. This strategy is best left when you have far more experience, but certainly not for people.

6. Focus only on penny stocks with high volume. They have higher chances of gaining a profit and success. Penny stocks that are traded more frequently and have a lot of activity is proof of higher liquidity.

7. Use mental stops. This is because the bid-ask spreads can potentially be high on penny stocks, and stop-losses can sometimes cause you to lose money from time to time. It is generally better to use mental stops.

8. Don't trade big. Basically, avoid the common pump and dump schemes that tend to circulate around penny stocks. A way to identify this is by discovering the reason why penny stocks earnings are rising. Again, if you find no clear

reason, it is likely to be a pump and dump scheme, where traders insert a large amount of money to inflate the sales, then sell all their stock, leaving the over-eager traders at a huge loss who jumped on board without double-checking their facts.

9. Don't fall in love with a stock. This means do not get emotionally attached to something you may have to let go of quickly. This may seem weird, but it is easy to get emotionally invested in something, especially if you spend a lot of time and research on a certain stock and possibly even the business itself. Companies market with an exciting story to keep you hooked, but this is exactly why you need to keep a personal distance from it all. Your strategy is to gain a profit, and sometimes it means letting go of stocks quickly and not taking part in whatever story they seem to be selling.

10. Finally, only buy the best of the bunch. Playing favoritism certainly works with penny stock investing, and it is best to purchase penny stocks that have had an earnings breakout. This is proof that companies are doing their job and are quite easy to find if you know where to look. Be aware of pump and dump schemes or scammers, as they can be mingled amongst the successful penny stocks.

10 Quick and Effective Tactics

Here are some of the proven and effective tactics you may want to consider when taking on penny stock investing. Keep in mind that you need to use these regarding what fits your circumstances best, or adapt them in such a way as is needed. These tactics are generic, and your scenarios are specific. Yet, it is handy to keep these tools at the ready and whip them out whenever you see an ideal scenario.

You can start off by calling the company. This does not mean to buy altogether what they are selling, but it is best to call a company you are indeed interested in investing in them. It is still ideal to also ask the necessary questions you may have, and verify if ever you can, and be in contact with some of the management or investor relations contact. You can still discover a lot about a company in a ten-to-twenty-minute phone call even after certain hours of research. But, again, be cautious, as it is best to filter what you can and see if you can verify what they tell you.

Average up, instead of averaging down. This is a common trick used by savvy investors, meaning they do tend to purchase more shares when their investments do happen to increase in price. When the first purchase is made, the rising prices instigate one's belief that there is greater potential for the company. Their position will increase when the stock rises because they averaged up, considering they did purchase more at a higher price. But who would mind paying for stocks that are moving in the right direction?

Many beginners in trading have the tendency of averaging down, which means they purchase shares when it starts to fall in value. Although the logic tends to focus on being able to buy a higher quantity, they lose sight of the fact that a share is not doing so well when the price starts to sink. So why would you want to buy more stock as its value is starting to fall? In this case, you are buying for a loss, especially considering you do not have a guarantee for it to turn around and head back up in value.

It is best not to mix up the market risk with company risk. There are two different risks involved when you are investing in any form of stock. They are company risk and market risk. Company risks normally involve anything that tends to be related to the stock of the corporation you happen to be investing in. Market risk is the downside of any shares and overall stock market declines. Basically, indirectly connected to the company you are invested in, but more a general risk that any trader is taking on. If there is an overall crash in the value of investments, then even the best-growing companies' share value will drop. There is practically nothing a company can do with this risk, as again, it is indirectly connected to them and depends on the direction of most companies and not simply theirs. This is something you must be aware of when investing in any company. There is the company risk and the overall risk of the market in its entirety. Now, this does not mean there is a ticking time bomb in the markets, but as shown before, it can happen.

Remember to try out the product and use the service of the company you are interested in investing in. Testing out a company's service or product is probably the most effective marketing research you can perform and can prove even more effective than analyzing the financial results of the business. This is especially important with penny stocks, as understanding how customers feel about a business can give a clear picture of how it could flourish or fail in the future. This way, you are also far more aware of the quality of the service they are selling or how well the product works. This can truly make or break a company, and so it is wise to be one step ahead in understanding whether they appeal to the market.

Study the competition. How a business can compete will also make or break a company. Businesses that have been successful for decades suddenly plummet because of their inability to stay up-to-date. The economy is extremely competitive, and with the rise of international businesses, many are not just competing on a local scale but also a global one. If businesses from international countries still work for cheaper or produce better products, time and again, the local products are bound to fail or decrease in size and value. Therefore, it is best to do your own research on how the competition is faring against the business you want to invest in. Looking up their competitive edge or how well they can keep themselves up-to-date is important in predicting their potential for success. This may seem like extra work, but it is necessary for penny stocks, where information is few and far between.

Again, paper trading. It is a tactic mentioned a few times, and one does not need to dive in too deeply, as the advantages have already been mentioned. You are just doing yourself a massive favor by diving in and using this tactic.

Even as a beginner, it is a great tactic to understand the life cycle of a corporate company. Being able to identify where the business is will help you to know whether you should even consider investing at this point and time.

All companies go through these cycles. It is inevitable. Many of them can extend a certain period within the business. However, history has proven this cycle time and again. Depending on the phase the company is in does depend on how you should treat its shares.

1. Start-up phase

2. Growth phase

3. Maturity phase

4. Decline phase

The positive side to this spectrum is that when a company does decline, it can always reinvent itself. By taking a step back, reevaluating, and adapting to begin the start-up phase again is normally what a good company does. A company needs to keep up with the competition, normally bringing something new and unique to the table.

Awareness of the corporate cycle will certainly go a long way for you to make the right investment decisions.

Finally, remember to take your time to understand what exactly is driving the share price. This may take some time to learn, but it should become easier. Remember to also monitor the short interest (the percentage of shares in a company that is held by short-sellers—the total number of shares that had finally been sold short by the investors, however, it had not yet been fully closed out or even covered). This is normally revealed in the form of a percentage. When it is shown in a percentage, it normally takes the shorted shares to the number of outstanding shares.

Shorting Stocks: What Does This Mean?

This normally refers to short selling, where the investment or trading strategy speculates that there is a decline in both stock and security prices. This is quite a complex strategy, best taken on by people who have had more experience when it comes to trading.

At the end of the day, all these trading tools and tactics are to help your journey along with penny stock trading, but it can never be an absolute guarantee. However, using these tactics can reduce a lot of mistakes and losses, and take your time incorporating them all. Also, respect yourself to the fact that you are completely new to all this, and it will take time to add everything you need to. So again, take your time, and remember to revisit the guides and books to brush up on anything that you may have forgotten.

Keep in mind that you are also a beginner, so when you choose your strategies and endgame, you must keep this in mind. Play the game of trades with a knowledge of your limitations, pushing yourself to become better and take on more tactics available in the trader's world. The more experience you build, the more profitable you are likely to become. Do not be afraid to push yourself, and just be aware when you cannot go any further, for now, anyway.

Conclusion

Now you know enough to kick-start your journey! Although there is truly so much more to learn, you now have the tools and equipment to discover it for yourself.

Penny stock investing is no easy feat, but it is not so insanely complex either. You may have noticed several key points that kept rising in the book, and they are indeed some solid factors that make or break your ultimate success.

As much as one can wish to guarantee that you will earn major profits, such promises are dangerous to make in the world of trade. But following this guide can certainly boost your potential, and that is a promise. Do not be afraid to revise or visit the guide again in order to brush up on forgotten facts and realities when it comes to penny stocks. Especially as you start out, repeating what you know and keeping the tactics sharp and fresh in your mind can help you make far healthier decisions. Additionally, keep the following in mind:

Do your research. Those three words are the main factors that help to make or break your trading career. Some follow others and simply earn by blind luck, only to suffer a loss or several losses if they continue to follow this pattern. Any savvy investor can tell you the key to standing out is by working for it. Even if it means doing five minutes of extra reading that most people would merely dismiss. This is where "doing your homework" pays off, and normally in a profitable way.

Remember the volatility and randomness in the market. It is best to be forgiving when you happen to fail an analysis, nor do things happen according to plan. As much as one could say that the market is fully predictable, that would be an outright lie. Accepting the randomness of the market, and preparing yourself emotionally, is building the stepping stones for a greater and longer trader's journey, where failure does not occur. Rather, these are mistakes that can be learned from.

Finally, never invest money you cannot afford to lose. This has been repeated more than once, but this is a factor you absolutely cannot ignore. Too many people have suffered by making this mistake; do not add your name to this list.

Keep in mind that penny stock investing requires a different approach to normal investing and traditionally is more hands-on. This means you will have to take more time and effort to earn profits in this category. In addition, this is a more volatile market, which means there is normally a greater amount of risk entailed to it. But the greater the risk, the greater the reward. However, be realistic about the level of profits that may stream in; otherwise, it may just lead to disappointment and giving up (which we certainly do not want).

Lastly, enjoy it! It is no use working an extensive and stressful journey in investing without finding some joy and happiness in the journey itself. So remember to keep smiling and cling to any form of positivity. Join a community of like-minded people, and do not be afraid to ask for their advice. However, remember they have their own biased views, and it would truly be best to filter between them for the rare gems that do come from people who have had experience.

Penny stock investing has small share prices with huge potential, and this is what you want to tap into. Practice having a trader's mentality when approaching this, and remember that you are not completely alone in this journey. Do not be afraid to adopt the strategies of others if you conclude they can work, and don't be afraid to stick to the plan or adapt it if circumstances do change.

At the end of the day, you are responsible for the income streaming your way. It is up to you and not the opinions of others to steer your investments forward. So, keep your chin up and stay up-to-date on the competition. It is best in the world of trading to stay ahead in the game, and that is something you should always be striving and working hard towards. Strive for growing and learning, not perfection, and you will already be far more ahead and aware than most traders. Penny stocks await you. So, are you ready to jump in today?

References

5 Best Penny Stocks To Buy Now & How to Develop a Strategy. (2017, September 20). Timothy Sykes. https://www.timothysykes.com/blog/best-penny-stocks/#How_to_Find_the_Best_Penny_Stocks_in_10_Steps

10 Rapid Result Tactics for Penny Stock Traders. (n.d.). Dummies. Retrieved July 31, 2021, from https://www.dummies.com/personal-finance/investing/penny-stocks/10-rapid-result-tactics-penny-stock-traders/

64 Penny Stock Trading Rules to Honor My $127,000 Profit Week. (2014, March 2). Timothy Sykes. https://www.timothysykes.com/blog/164-penny-stock-trading-rulestips-celebrate-164000-profit-week/

Advantages & Disadvantages of Penny Stock. (n.d.). Pocketsense. Retrieved July 31, 2021, from https://pocketsense.com/advantages-disadvantages-penny-stock-3471.html

Balance, F. B. F. L. P. L. wrote about penny stocks for T., Books, I. the A. of T., & Leeds, including "Penny S. for D. "R. T. B. editorial policies P. (n.d.). *Here Is a Step-By-Step Guide How to Get Started Trading Penny Stocks*. The Balance. https://www.thebalance.com/penny-stocks-trading-guide-for-beginners-4123635

Beginners Penny Stock Trading Strategy (momo). (2016, November 14). Warrior Trading. https://www.warriortrading.com/penny-stock-trading/

Buying Penny Stocks [Understanding Penny Stocks].
(n.d.). Www.pennystocks.org. Retrieved July 31, 2021,
from http://www.pennystocks.org/buying-penny-stocks.php

Curtis, G. (2020, April 4). *Trading psychology: Why the
mind matters in making money*. Investopedia.
https://www.investopedia.com/articles/trading/02/110502.a
sp

*Day Trading Tools | Penny Stock Tools & Resources |
ClayTrader*. (n.d.). Retrieved July 31, 2021, from
https://claytrader.com/resources/

*Emotional Trading: These 7 Emotions Can Destroy Your
Dream! - DTTW*. (2021, May 28). Day Trade the WorldTM.
https://www.daytradetheworld.com/trading-blog/these-7-
emotions-can-destroy-your-day-trading-dream/

finance, F. B. F. T. P. N. writes about all aspects of
personal, Retirement, I. S. for, Wisely, I., & Nolan, being a
smart consumer R. T. B. editorial policies P. (n.d.). *What
Is a Penny Stock?* The Balance. Retrieved July 30, 2021,
from https://www.thebalance.com/what-is-a-penny-stock-
5114192

*Getting a Good StockBroker [Understanding Penny
Stocks]*. (n.d.). Www.pennystocks.org. Retrieved July 31,
2021, from http://www.pennystocks.org/getting-a-good-
stock-broker.php

*Getting Started in Penny Stocks [Understanding Penny
Stocks]*. (n.d.). Www.pennystocks.org. Retrieved July 31,
2021, from http://www.pennystocks.org/getting-started-in-
penny-stocks.php

Glossary of Terms Used [Understanding Penny Stocks].
(n.d.). Www.pennystocks.org.
http://www.pennystocks.org/glossary-of-terms-used.php

Guides, T. S. (2019). Penny Stocks for Beginners. Trading With Just $100. *Tradingstrategyguides.com*. https://tradingstrategyguides.com/penny-stocks/

Hayes, A. (n.d.). *Candlestick*. Investopedia. https://www.investopedia.com/terms/c/candlestick.asp

Hayes, A. (2019). *A Breakdown on How the Stock Market Works*. Investopedia. https://www.investopedia.com/articles/investing/082614/how-stock-market-works.asp

How (and Where) To Find Penny Stocks To Buy. (n.d.). Wall Street Survivor. Retrieved July 31, 2021, from https://www.wallstreetsurvivor.com/starter-guides/find-penny-stock/

How To Day Trade Penny Stocks & 9 Important Strategies To Learn Now. (2021, January 31). Penny Stocks to Buy, Picks, News and Information | PennyStocks.com. https://pennystocks.com/featured/2021/01/31/how-to-trade-penny-stocks-9-important-strategies-to-learn-now/

How to Find Penny Stocks Pre-Spike (Step-by-Step Guide). (2019, June 26). Timothy Sykes. https://www.timothysykes.com/blog/my-secret-formula-for-finding-penny-stocks-pre-spike/#How_to_Pick_a_Potential_Penny_Stock_Winner_Pre-Spike-2

How To Invest In Penny Stocks - The Complete Step By Step Guide. (n.d.). Money under 30. Retrieved July 31, 2021, from https://www.moneyunder30.com/how-to-invest-in-penny-stocks

Investor Bulletin: Microcap Stock Basics (Part 1 of 3: General Information) | Investor.gov. (n.d.). Www.investor.gov. Retrieved July 30, 2021, from https://www.investor.gov/introduction-investing/general-resources/news-alerts/alerts-bulletins/investor-bulletins/investor-3

Investor Bulletin: Microcap Stock Basics (Part 2 of 3: Research) | Investor.gov. (n.d.). Www.investor.gov. Retrieved July 31, 2021, from https://www.investor.gov/introduction-investing/general-resources/news-alerts/alerts-bulletins/investor-bulletins-32

Keythman, B. (n.d.). *How to Compare Market Capitalization & Stockholders' Equity.* Finance - Zacks. Retrieved July 31, 2021, from https://finance.zacks.com/compare-market-capitalization-stockholders-equity-1812.html

Murphy, C. B. (2021, January 28). *How Penny Stocks Trade and How Investors Can Buy Them.* Investopedia. https://www.investopedia.com/terms/p/pennystock.asp

Penny Stock Chart Patterns Every Trader Should Know [Top 5]. (2019, June 19). Penny Stocks to Buy, Picks, News and Information | PennyStocks.com. https://pennystocks.com/featured/2019/06/19/penny-stock-chart-patterns-every-trader-should-know-top-5/

Penny Stocks for Day Trading: Beginner's Guide. (2020, December 23). StocksToTrade. https://stockstotrade.com/penny-stocks-for-day-trading/#Things_I_Look_for_in_Penny_Stocks_for_Day_Trading

Penny Stocks Trading Guide for Beginners [2020]. (2016, December 22). Warrior Trading. https://www.warriortrading.com/penny-stocks/

Should You Invest or Trade Penny Stocks? - Pros & Cons Of Penny Stocks. (2020, October 27). Rockwell Trading. https://www.rockwelltrading.com/coffee-with-markus/should-you-invest-in-penny-stocks/

Sincere, M. (n.d.). *10 ways to trade penny stocks*. MarketWatch. Retrieved July 31, 2021, from https://www.marketwatch.com/story/10-ways-to-trade-penny-stocks-2012-02-03

Step by Step Penny Stock Guide. (n.d.). Www.peterleeds.com. Retrieved July 31, 2021, from https://www.peterleeds.com/step-by-step-penny-stock-guide.htm

Stockopedia - Stock Screening, Ratings, & Portfolio Analysis. (n.d.). Stockopedia. Retrieved July 31, 2021, from http://www.stockopedia.com

stocks, F. B. F. L. P. L. is an expert on investing in, Planning, H. O. a D. of E. W. with F., derivatives, equities, Income, F., Management, P., Dummies, analytics H. is the author of several publications including "Penny S. for, Stocks, publishes the financial newsletter P. L. P., NBC, CBS, Fox, CNN, Today, R., & Leeds, several dozen other outlets P. attended the U. of W. R. T. B. editorial policies P. (n.d.). *Pros and Cons of Penny Stock Investing*. The Balance. https://www.thebalance.com/the-pros-and-cons-of-penny-stocks-2637072

The First Deadly Sin Of The Penny Stock Trader: Greed. (n.d.). Www.meta-Formula.com. Retrieved July 31, 2021, from https://www.meta-formula.com/penny-stock-trader.html

The Pros and Cons of Trading Penny Stocks. (2019, May 31). Modest Money. https://www.modestmoney.com/pros-cons-trading-penny-stocks/

Trading Psychology: How to Get Into a Successful Mindset. (2018, February 28). Timothy Sykes. https://www.timothysykes.com/blog/improve-trading-psychology

trading, F. B. F. L. F. T. C. M. is a financial writer with over 13 years experience creating markets-related content H. is an expert in, Analysis, T., & Murphy, C. received a bachelor's degree in finance from the U. of A. L. about our editorial policies C. (n.d.). *How to Invest in Penny Stocks for Beginners.* Investopedia. Retrieved July 31, 2021, from https://www.investopedia.com/articles/investing/091114/how-invest-penny-stocks.asp

Where Do Penny Stocks Trade? [Understanding Penny Stocks]. (n.d.). Www.pennystocks.org. Retrieved July 31, 2021, from http://www.pennystocks.org/where-do-penny-stocks-trade.php

Why Trade Penny Stocks? 4 Simple Reasons Why. (2018, December 13). StocksToTrade. https://stockstotrade.com/why-trade-penny-stocks/

Yahoo Finance - Business Finance, Stock Market, Quotes, News. (2015). @YahooFinance. http://finance.yahoo.com

Image Referencing:

AbsolutVision. (n.d.). *No Risk No Reward.*
https://Pixabay.com/Illustrations/Dices-Over-Newspaper-
Profit-2656028/.

Chen, J. (2019). *Penny Stocks Short Selling.*
Investopedia.
https://www.investopedia.com/terms/s/shortselling.asp

Hassan, M. (n.d.-a). *Candle Charts.*
https://Pixabay.com/Vectors/Business-Forex-Stock-Chart-
Trading-5477997/.

Hassan, M. (n.d.-b). *Stay Focused.*
https://Pixabay.com/Illustrations/Visa-Virtual-Visa-Credit-
Card-3349340/.

Hassan, M. (n.d.-c). *You Need A Plan.*
https://Pixabay.com/Vectors/Training-Course-Business-
Session-5822607/.

Mediamodifier. (n.d.). *Downside of Penny Stocks -Graph
Growth Process.* https://Pixabay.com/Illustrations/Graph-
Growth-Progress-Diagram-3078546/.

Openartclipvectors. (n.d.). *Do's and Dont's.*
https://Pixabay.com/Vectors/Business-Commerce-
Decisions-1297332/.

OpenClipart Vectors. (n.d.). *Trader Toolbox.*
https://Pixabay.com/Vectors/Briefcase-Toolbox-Box-Tools-
157280/.

OpenClipartvectors. (n.d.). *Research is Key*.
https://Pixabay.com/Vectors/Papers-Stack-Heap-
Documents-576385/.

Tumisu. (n.d.). *Mental Battle of a Trader*.
https://Pixabay.com/Illustrations/Mental-Health-
Psychology-Psychiatry-2313428/.

ALGORITHMIC TRADING

Step-By-Step Guide to Develop Your Own Winning Trading Strategy Using Financial Machine Learning Without Having to Learn Code

Investors Press

Introduction

"I have two basic rules about winning in trading as well as in life: 1) If you don't bet, you can't win. 2) If you lose all your chips, you can't bet."

-by Larry Hite

For decades, stock trading was locked behind the door of wealth and exclusivity. When that door opened with the introduction of online trading platforms and discount brokers, a flood of new investors and traders entered the market exchange.

In many ways, the introduction of discount brokers and online trading platforms was a breath of fresh air. It opened up the market and boosted our global economy. It also gave everyone with a bit of cash and an internet connection the opportunity to grow their wealth.

However, when you're just starting out in trading and investment, the world of financial investments can be quite overwhelming, especially if you're starting without much guidance, which is the case with discount brokers.

After all, as a newbie, how do you know what to invest in, how to invest, and when to invest? Well, when embarking on any new venture, the first thing most of us tend to do is jump into some research.

In the time before Google, research often meant pouring over large texts and getting yourself dusty in the library. We're glad to say that those days are long gone.

With increasingly sophisticated technological advancements, trading no longer needs to be a daunting task. These days, there are paper trading accounts and online webinars, all of which are aimed at helping beginners land on their feet.

When you've traversed the financial markets for a bit, you'll be exposed to a plethora of trading techniques, methods, and strategies that you can use when interacting with financial markets. These methods and strategies come in all shapes and sizes and are suited toward every level of expertise there is.

If you're a bit more tech-savvy and are looking to jump into trading and investment, algorithmic trading might be the perfect way to navigate the financial market.

If you're reading this book, chances are pretty high that you've heard about algorithmic trading and are interested in exploring it as a possible avenue of trade and investment.

But, as with all things concerning finance, you know that you should be doing your research before jumping in.

That's where we come in.

This book is aimed at discussing the basics of algorithmic trading and helping you use algo trading as a means of managing your investment portfolio. We're here to answer questions like whether algo trading is better than manual trading and if algo trading even works.

In short, this book is a crash course on algorithmic trading and covers things like the basics of algo trading, its uses, risks and benefits, and how to get started.

It also includes a basic how-to on developing algorithmic strategies, the best practices that you should implement when starting out, and it offers additional resources that you can check out once you've gained all you need to from this book.

Who Is Investors Press? And Why Should You Trust Us?

Now, we know what you're thinking. Who is this author? And what do they know about finance and trading?

And you're absolutely within your rights to ask these questions. Well, we are the team behind Investors Press, a publishing company that specializes in providing resources for traders and investors.

We've studied asset trading and have done extensive research along with experts on the different topics we tackle, and we hope that our experience will help you achieve success in your trading and investing journey. We've done a thorough and exhaustive study on algorithmic trading, and we think that, if you're willing to rise to the challenge, it could be a great tool to add to your arsenal.

We wrote this book to act as a useful resource for beginners and to simplify the complex topic of algorithmic trading. We also intended this book to act as a guide to help beginners navigate the world of trading.

Chapter Overview

Before we jump in, here's a brief overview of what this book offers:

Chapter 1 acts as an introduction to algorithmic trading. This chapter covers the basics of algorithmic trading, how it works, and how it's used by traders and investors.

Chapter 2 discusses what you'll need to know and what you'll need to learn in order to start implementing algorithmic trading. In this chapter, we'll cover the kind of equipment and software you'll need, as well as the skills you'll need to acquire.

Chapter 3 breaks down the steps to start algorithmic trading and covers things like how to develop your own algorithm and trading strategy. It also focuses on helping you test algorithms and strategies.

Chapter 4 presents common trading strategies that are used in algorithmic trading. It also provides tips on how to find trading and arbitrage opportunities.

Chapter 5 focuses on helping you keep your algorithm up-to-date and relevant, which is particularly important given how quickly the market shifts. This chapter also provides tips on how to evaluate your trading strategy in order to maintain efficiency.

Chapter 6 takes a look at risk management and aims to help you identify the risks that come along with algorithmic trading and how to manage them.

Lastly, **Chapter 7** outlines additional resources that you can access if you'd like to further your knowledge on algorithmic trading. In this chapter we've also added the links to these resources if you'd like to jump right in.

Now that you know what you're in for, let's jump in!

Chapter 1:
Basics of Algorithmic Trading

Algorithmic trading is one of the many methods of traversing through financial markets. But, like most trading methods, implementing algorithmic trading and turning it into a viable investment method takes time, patience, and practice.

And, like most trading methods, algorithmic trading requires a unique set of skills. In addition to being well versed in trade and investments, you'll also need to be able to code and program.

But, before we get into the logistics of algorithmic trading, you need to know the basics first.

What is Algorithmic Trading

So, what is algorithmic trading?

In simple terms, algorithmic trading (also known as automated trading) makes use of a computer program that has been given a series of instructions to place a trade. At its core, algorithmic trading is a systematic approach to financial trading.

The computer program, when making use of these instructions (algorithm), can execute trades at a speed and frequency that we humans aren't able to reach. The computer program is based on a mathematical equation, or algorithm, that lays out a defined set of instructions on how the program needs to behave (Seth, 2021).

These instructions include specifics such as which financial instrument to trade, the price points to trade at, and the quantity that should be traded. These algorithms often consist of complex formulas in combination with mathematical models (Chen, 2019). However, while algorithmic trading is automated, it still requires human intervention, particularly given how often financial trends and markets shift.

Due to the automated function which defines algorithmic trading, this method is often used by high volume, high-frequency traders.

Algorithmic trading emerged in the mid-1970s, when the New York Stock Exchange introduced the Designated Order Turnaround (DOT) system. The DOT system involved routing orders from the traders to specialists who were located on the exchange floor (Chen, 2019).

You must remember, in the mid-1970s, the luxury of online trading hadn't yet reared its head, and thus, trade exchanges were often physical locations.

As the years passed and technology improved, electronic trading gained prevalence and, by 2009, over 60% of all trades in the United States were executed electronically (Chen, 2019). These days, electronic trading has become widespread. Discount brokers, and online brokers, are increasingly commonplace.

Algorithmic trading is no exception. There are tons of programmers who write code for algorithmic trading as a means of earning extra income. However, with the prevalence of high-speed internet and fast computers, algorithmic trading is a skill almost anyone can pick up.

With the introduction of artificial intelligence (AI) and machine learning, computer programmers are now able to create algorithms that can improve and update themselves through a process called deep learning. This lessens the need for human intervention and allows the algorithm to adapt to market trends (Chen, 2019).

However, as much as technology has revolutionized financial trade, we would still advise that you keep your eye on your trade and investment profiles when using automated systems such as algorithmic trading.

How Does Algorithmic Trading Work?

As we've mentioned, algorithmic trading is, in essence, a computer program that follows instructions.

For example, let's say you set up a program that has been instructed to:

1. Buy 20 shares of stock once the 50-day moving average exceeds the 200-day moving average.

2. Sell shares whose 50-day moving average shifts below the 200-day moving average.

Now, this is a pretty simple set of instructions, and the computer will trade based on these instructions. The program automatically monitors the stock price of the shares and waits for the moving average of these shares to meet the criteria set out by the instructions before executing a trade.

Now, this might seem overly simplistic, and that's because it is. Algorithmic trading entails much more than just creating a computer program to do all your trading for you. Merely creating a program doesn't mean that it'll be effective at boosting your income.

Algorithmic trading takes work to, well, work.

In order to make algorithmic trading a profitable and viable trading option, you need to do the following:

- Find a trading strategy that works for you and matches your financial goals

- Create an algorithm that suits your trading strategy

- Test your algorithm extensively to make sure that it works as intended

- Create a trading and investment portfolio

- And lastly, monitor and evaluate your algorithm and strategy in order to ensure that it's effective

And that's just the basics!

Now, we're not trying to scare you. While technology has made trading easier, you'll still need to do your due diligence. With something as complex as algorithmic trading, it'll take a lot more than just research.

Before you panic, let's take a breath. This is a beginner's guide, and we'll be helping you through each and every step along the way.

Finding a Trading Strategy

Having an effective trading strategy is the cornerstone of every algorithmic trader. Without a proper strategy, you won't be able to implement an effective algorithm.

The first step when pursuing trade and investment is to find a trading strategy that aligns with your needs and financial goals. The first step toward deciding on a trading strategy is knowing your financial situation and clearly defining your financial goals. You should also consider aspects like how much time you have to spend on trading and the amount of money you want to trade.

Remember, the strategy you choose should be in line with what you'd like to achieve. The entire purpose of a trading strategy is to help you achieve your financial goals.

Now, you have two options here. You could try to develop your own trading strategy or implement one of the many trading strategies that exist within the world of finance. If you're a beginner at trading and trading strategies, we would suggest you check out pre-existing strategies.

However, for interest's sake, let's go over the steps to creating your own strategy. We'll be covering algorithmic trading strategies in Chapter 4.

Creating Your Own Trading Strategy

Before you're able to begin defining your trading strategy, you need to outline a few basic tenets.

Firstly, what financial instrument do you want to trade? Are you focused more on stocks or commodities? Perhaps you'd like to trade futures contracts or options?

The financial instrument you decide to trade will heavily influence your strategy. After all, trading stocks is slightly different than trading options or commodities. If you're a beginner, we would suggest starting with one financial instrument. Once you've become more comfortable and familiar with trading you can branch out and begin diversifying your investment portfolio.

After you've chosen a financial instrument, it's time to come up with a trading idea.

1. **The Idea:** Your trading idea can be anything from wanting to do high volume trades or trading casually. The point is that this idea will form the basis of your strategy (Samuelsson, 2021).

During this phase, you can be as creative and innovative as you want to be. The only limitation is your own imagination.

When you come up with your idea, we would suggest browsing trading forums for inspiration.

2. **Backtesting:** Now that you've come up with your trading idea, you need to figure out if it's viable. The easiest way to do this is by 'backtesting' the idea. Basically, this entails testing your newly formed trading strategy on historical data in order to see if the strategy will work or not.

Backtesting relies heavily on the 'equity curve.' The equity curve is a visual representation of market trends and the variation of the value of trade and investment accounts over a period of time (Burns, 2020). This is generally shown via a graph.

An upward equity curve means that the trading strategy being used is profitable over time. A downward curve means that your trading strategy doesn't line up with market trends and is unlikely to be profitable.

Backtesting uses the equity curve to gauge the viability of a trading strategy by focusing on specific buy and sell signals, like the instructions mentioned above.

While backtesting is a great preliminary test for your trading strategy, we would suggest you take it a step further by employing 'robustness testing.'

3. **Robustness Testing:** More often than not, backtesting isn't enough to ensure the viability of a trading strategy. We like to think about backtesting as a preliminary indicator of whether you're on the right track in developing a strategy or not.

   After all, the only thing that backtesting shows is that your trading strategy is suited to random market babble. It's not a true test of whether your trading strategy will match up to true market trends and behavior.

   Robustness testing, also known as stress testing, means putting your trading strategy through various tests, each of which changes certain variables, such as the price data (Bryant, n.d.).

   If your trading strategy is 'robust,' it will have relatively muted reactions to the changes in variables, whereas if it's not, it will react disproportionally. In some cases, your trading strategy might fail completely.

   The aim here is to give you some idea of how your trading strategy might react in live market conditions. If your trading strategy is unable to handle these changes effectively, chances are, it won't survive in true market conditions.

Conducting stress testing is very important because real-time markets are in a constant state of flux. Robustness testing aims to emulate the constant changes in market trends in order to ensure that the strategy will be able to handle them. It focuses on finding out how your trading strategy will perform once market conditions are no longer ideal (Bryant, n.d.).

4. **Creating Your Portfolio:** Now that you've developed and tested your trading strategy, it's time to create a portfolio of strategies.

   It's common practice for experienced traders to have various investment and trade portfolios, each operating on a different trade strategy and often with a different financial instrument.

   What makes algorithmic trading so great is that it allows you to run numerous portfolios and strategies at once. Having diversified portfolios running numerous trading strategies is also a great way to protect yourself from risk (Samuelsson, 2021).

   This is because if one of the portfolios and strategies fails, you'll have multiple backups and you'll be able to mitigate the loss. Having multiple strategies in place also allows you to adapt easily to market shifts.

While this method of trade is ideal, we wouldn't suggest it to beginners. Having a wide range of portfolios (hopefully a diverse set) can become complicated to manage, especially if you're a beginner and are still finding your feet.

For beginners, we would suggest starting with a single portfolio that follows one trade strategy and focuses on one financial instrument.

5. **Monitoring the Strategies:** Now that your portfolio is all set up, the real fun begins. It's time to monitor the strategy or strategies that you've implemented.

   Now, depending on how much time you have on hand, as well as the intensity of your trade strategy, this could take anywhere from a few minutes to a couple of hours. If you're pressed for time, we would suggest implementing a simple strategy that's easy to keep track of.

   While it can be tempting to leave the algorithm to run your portfolio for you, you should keep in mind that algorithmic trading requires a fair bit of monitoring to ensure that it's working optimally.

   Monitoring your strategy allows you to pick up on any errors in the code or instructions that you might've missed. It also allows you to make sure that your connection hasn't disconnected from the server.

This strategy is one of the things that will ensure that you're able to mitigate any risks that could come from software or hardware malfunction.

However, this doesn't mean that you'll have to be glued to your PC for hours at a time. These days, it's possible to check your trading via a remote server. This allows you to check on your portfolio from your cellphone if you find yourself away from home.

How is Algorithmic Trading Used?

Thus far, we've discussed the basics of what algorithmic trading is and how it works, but how is this method used? Well, there are numerous forms of trading that could make use of algorithmic trading.

Remember, algorithmic trading is a systematic approach to active trading and can be used in nearly every form of trade, depending on how it's programmed (Chen, 2019).

In this section, we'll be going over three common trade and investment activities that could use algorithmic trading:

1. **Short-term traders,** market makers, speculators, and sell-side participants often benefit from automated trade executions. With regard to market makers, the addition of algorithmic traders also aids in keeping financial markets sufficiently liquid for buyers and sellers.

Liquidity within financial markets is especially important because it allows the market to function as intended. That is to say that it allows quick and easy trade and investments.

2. Algorithmic trading is also used by mid-term and long-term investors and buy-side firms. In this case, algorithmic trading is used to buy large amounts of stocks without influencing market trends and stock prices. This type of algorithmic trading allows traders and investors to make discrete, high-volume trades and investments.

3. More commonly, algorithmic trading is used by systematic traders, who tend to follow market trends. This could include hedge fund traders or pair traders.

   Systematic traders will often prefer to automate their trades according to a set of instructions rather than trading manually, due to the efficiency of automatic trading.

While algorithmic trading is a versatile and effective method of trade and investment, it does not suit every financial market. For example, algorithmic trading works best with financial instruments such as stocks, ETFs, highly liquid futures contracts, and forex pairs.

In essence, algorithmic trading works best in highly liquid financial markets due to the large trading volume and speed associated with automatic trading.

The Advantages and Disadvantages of Algorithmic Trading

There are numerous advantages and disadvantages of algorithmic trading. Before you run full speed ahead with algo trading, it's important that you understand the risks as well as the benefits associated with it.

The Benefits of Algo Trading

Algorithmic trading is often used by large brokerage firms and institutional investors in order to cut down on the costs associated with trading. Studies have shown that algorithmic trading is particularly useful for high-volume traders.

The major benefit of algorithmic trading is that it's often used to increase market liquidity, which allows financial markets to operate as intended.

Additional benefits include:

Speed

By now, you must have realized that a major benefit of algorithmic trading is that it allows for faster and easier trade executions. Due to the trade speed and volume that algorithmic trading allows, it's ideal for scalp trading.

Scalp trading involves profiting from small price fluctuations that occur over a period of time by rapidly buying and selling financial assets at small price increments (Laster, n.d.).

Algorithmic trading also allows you to execute trades based on numerous indicators at speeds that humans often can't reach. This allows you to analyze and execute trades faster, and it provides you with more trading opportunities (Laster, n.d.).

However, while speed is a major benefit to algorithmic trading, it can become an issue if a large number of trades are executed over an extended period of time without human intervention. As mentioned in the previous section, monitoring your trades and trade profile is vitally important to ensure that you don't incur unnecessary losses.

Accuracy

As with everything in finance, accuracy is very important in trading and investments. This is especially true given market trends and fluctuations. Given your level of expertise and experience, you might be able to accurately execute trades at high volumes without much issue.

However, unless you're a professional investor, this level of trade is often inaccessible to the layman trader.

Algorithmic trading often increases the accuracy of trades and reduces mistakes that could arise due to human error (Laster, n.d.). For example, if you're trading manually, you might accidentally buy or sell the wrong asset or buy and sell at the wrong price.

You might also be influenced to make certain trades because of the emotional state you're in. Some days you might feel more reckless and other days you might feel more cautious.

Algorithmic trading eliminates the effects of human emotion and acts only as it has been instructed. It's both predictable and reliable. It's also very effective at mitigating human error.

As discussed in the previous section, algorithmic trading also avoids human error by allowing for backtesting and robustness testing (Laster, n.d.). This allows you to test your algorithm and ensure that it will work the way you intended it to.

By mitigating human error, algorithmic trading also decreases the risks associated with trading manually.

Reduced Costs

As mentioned above, algorithmic trading is often used as a means of reducing the costs associated with trade and investment. Traders won't need to spend hours checking and rechecking markets as trade occurs since trading can be done without your supervision.

This allows you to cut down on costs and reduce the amount of time you'd normally spend trading if you did them manually. This gives you the freedom to spend your time as you choose, without being chained to your PC.

The Disadvantages of Algorithmic Trading

While algorithmic trading comes with numerous advantages, it also carries its fair share of disadvantages and risks. It's important to understand the disadvantages associated with algorithmic trading before jumping in.

Technical Errors

One of the biggest disadvantages of algorithmic trading is experiencing technical errors. After all, algorithmic trading is dependent on running specific software, having access to certain hardware, and being able to program the algorithm effectively.

Issues such as power failures, disconnecting servers, and software and hardware crashes are all risks associated with algorithmic trading.

If a power failure occurs or you lose your internet connection, trades will fail to be sent to the market and will go unexecuted; this could lead to losses.

There could also be a misalignment between projected trades generated by the algorithm and the actual trades executed if your hardware or software isn't up to standard.

Algorithmic trading is extremely technical, and there will be a steep learning curve when you're starting out. In addition to the skills you'll need to pick up, algorithmic trading also requires certain equipment, hardware, and software in order to operate. We discuss the hardware and software requirements of algorithmic trading in Chapter 2.

Over-Optimization

With algorithmic trading, you run the risk of developing a trading strategy that looks great on paper but ultimately fails in real-time market exchanges. What we mean by this is that your trading strategy might work well when backtesting but could still fail when introduced to real-time markets.

This is known as over-optimization. If your trading strategy is over-optimized, it'll exhibit excessive curve-fitting that excels in back-testing but is unable to keep up in live trading.

A good way to avoid over-optimization is to subject your trading strategy to numerous stress tests in order to see how it might behave when subjected to live trading. Even then, we would suggest trying your trading strategy with paper trading accounts in order to see if it'll be able to stand up against real-time market trends.

Paper trading accounts are a great resource for testing new trading strategies in simulated market exchanges. They're commonly offered by discount and online brokers.

Should You Shift From Manual Trading to Algorithmic Trading?

In general, there are two basic ways that you can interact with financial market exchanges. The first, which we have been discussing, is algorithmic or automated trading.

As we've discussed, automated trading is dependent on an algorithm and certain software. It requires very little human intervention and runs as the algorithm intends.

The second way is via manual trading. Manual trading is the more 'traditional' means of trading and has been around since the emergence of financial trade and investments. Manual trading, as the name implies, means trading as you want without the intervention of an algorithm. You decide when, where, and how to trade.

Every decision made comes from you.

Before we get into whether you should forgo manual trading for algo trading, let's take a look at the ins and outs of manual trading and all that it entails.

Manual Trading

Manual trading is, in essence, hands-on trading. You, as the trader, will personally execute trades and investments. This often means having to read market trends and price point fluctuations to see if they match your strategy and then deciding whether or not to execute a trade.

If you've decided to go through with the trade, you'll have to do it manually.

Nothing is automated.

Manual trading means that most of the work is done by the trader. Therefore, your output will only be as good as your input. How much profit you make will be determined by how many successful trades you're able to execute, as well as how quickly you're able to execute them, and how much time you have to spend dedicated to trading and investment.

Benefits to Manual Trading

Here are a few benefits to manual trading:

- Manual trading helps traders and investors adapt to and learn more about the financial market that they're interacting with. It also helps you familiarize yourself with the tools, graphs, and methods used when making trades. For example, these are technical and fundamental analysis tools.

  If you're a beginner in trading, manual trading is a great way to wrap your head around the ins and outs of trading and all the variables that influence market prices and fluctuations.

  If you're looking to build your knowledge, manual trading is the way to go.

- Manual trading gives you absolute control over your trades and investments. It also allows you full control of your portfolio management. This is great if you're working in live market exchanges because you make all the decisions.

  You decide where and how to spend your money when trading and investing.

- Manual trading also allows you to quickly figure out whether a trading strategy is working for you and identify little variables that need tweaking in order to improve your strategy.

166

You're also able to quickly identify weaknesses and mistakes in your trading strategy since you'll be working with it hands-on.

This allows you to quickly alter your trading strategy and mitigate preventable losses.

Drawbacks to Manual Trading

Here are a few common drawbacks to using manual trading:

- The biggest drawback to manual trading is that it takes time. You'll need to do your own research, place your orders and trades based on this research, read market trends, keep track of financial news, and spend a good deal of time reviewing your trade strategies to assess their efficiency and profitability.

  This takes time and an extensive amount of effort and energy. While a few of these steps can be automated, and most online brokers have streamlined their platforms to make this easier, it'll still require you to carve out time in your day to focus on your portfolio.

- Manual trading requires a lot of discipline and self-restraint in order to be successful. This means that you can't let your emotions influence your trading and investments.

  Oftentimes, you might feel compelled to execute certain trades because you're scared of missing out on 'the next big thing' or because you feel pressured by other traders. This could cause you to begin 'gambling' with your trades instead of executing them according to a sound strategy.

This opens you up to unnecessary risks and losses.

- Manual trading also comes with the disadvantage of falling prey to human error. We're all human, and thus we're prone to making mistakes. Trading is no exception. You could sell the wrong asset or invest in the wrong stock with a simple tap of a button.

This could cause you unnecessary losses.

Knowing that you caused yourself a loss can also be difficult to come to terms with. In fact, many traders struggle with being solely accountable for their portfolios.

Manual Trading vs. Algorithmic Trading

So, which method should you go with? Manual trading or algorithmic trading?

Well, the answer to that question is kind of complicated.

Firstly, we'd like to ask you what you wish to achieve with trading and investment, what your financial goals are, and why you would want to trade and invest.

If you can answer these, the next question becomes how involved you would like to be: would you prefer a hands-on approach, or would you prefer a more relaxed approach?

How much time do you have?

The method you choose needs to suit your needs, wants, and lifestyle. It would be easy for us to sit here and say *go with manual trading!* Or *go with automated trading!* But the truth is, the decision lies with you.

If you're reading this book, the chances are that you've already made your decision and have chosen to go with algorithmic trading. This means that you want a bit more freedom, a little less control, and a more systematic approach when it comes to trade.

That being said, just because you go with algorithmic trading now doesn't mean that manual trading is closed to you. If you have the time and energy, you could have it all.

Chapter 2:
Algorithmic Trading
Requirements

In the days of the old, trades and investments were reserved for the elite of society; but with the introduction of online and discount brokers, this has changed.

Now, anyone with a cell phone and internet connection can access financial markets for trades and investments. Beginners will still need to learn a few valuable skills; like being able to read market trends, make market predictions, and test out various trade methods in order to make successful trades, but it's all within reach.

However, unlike most trading and investing methods, algorithmic trading requires a bit more than just an internet connection and basic trading knowledge. If you want to be proficient in algorithmic trading and make it a viable trading option, you'll need to know how to program your algorithm and the hardware and software to run the algorithm.

This chapter discusses what you'll need to know and learn in order to start algorithmic trading. It also goes into the equipment you'll need (yes, algorithmic training requires specific hardware) and the software requirements.

The first section of this chapter covers the technical requirements (hardware) of algorithmic trading. The second focuses on the software you'll need to operate the algorithm, and the third focuses on identifying trading platforms that are ideal for algorithmic trading.

The last few sections of this chapter focus on the knowledge and skills you'll need to acquire, such as programming and the basics of trade, as well as a few tips on programming for beginners.

By the end of this chapter, you should have some idea of what you'll need to get started in algorithmic trading.

Hardware Requirements

Given that algorithm trading is made possible by using a computer program, one of the main hardware components you'll need is a computer. Now, if you think that your laptop will cut it, you're wrong.

Most mainstream and even gaming laptops won't be able to handle the pressure of running the program, software, and making trades without running the risk of overheating and crashing.

Instead, if you're looking to get into algorithmic trading, we suggest you invest in a 'trading computer.' Regardless of whether you're into day trading, swing trading, or algorithmic trading, a trading computer is a must.

Now, a 'trading computer' isn't some magical machine that'll turn you into a trading genius. It's a simple mid-range desktop computer that can be able to handle the software and programs you need to run without overheating or crashing and is used primarily for trading.

While a trading computer isn't much different from a normal computer, there are a few spec-specific features you need be focused on if you plan to build or buy a trading PC:

The CPU

The first thing you should be focusing on when buying or building a trading PC is the CPU. The CPU is the central processing unit and is present in nearly every electronic device, such as computers, cell phones, smart watches, e-readers, and even your thermostat. The CPU is in charge of processing and executing all instructions given to it. In many ways, it acts as the brain of the device.

Therefore, the faster the CPU is able to process and execute instructions, the faster your PC will be able to run. This will increase the speed at which the algorithm will be able to execute trades (Samuelsson, 2019).

With algorithmic trading, the difference between a fast and slow CPU is quite stark, and having a slow CPU could cost you. Having a fast CP also speeds up the trading process and frees up more time for research and strategy development (Samuelsson, 2019).

Now, when choosing a CPU, there's one key thing you should consider, and that's whether to go for a single core or multicore CPU.

Simply put: a single-core processor has one core, while multicore processors have numerous small processors that have been packed into a single chip.

In theory, multicore CPUs are much faster than single-core CPUs. Since their introduction in 2001, multicore CPUs have gained mass popularity, and these days most mainstream computers come with 16-32 cores.

However, multicore CPUs are not without their limitations. More often than not, trading platforms struggle to use all cores effectively (Samuelsson, 2019). Some trading platforms are better at handling multicore processors, and there's been a shift toward platforms increasing their support capabilities.

Given the rapid improvements in technology, we would suggest you go for a multicore CPU. The chances are that most trading platforms will update their software in order to keep up with the times.

The Graphics Card

For most PC users, purchasing a fancy graphics card isn't something that they think about. When many start out in trading, getting a trading PC and a high-end graphics card never crossed their minds. Many assume it was something only high-end gamers needed.

How far from the truth that was.

These days, graphics cards are not only used by gamers and video editors, but also by crypto traders in order to mine cryptocurrency, and you guessed it, algorithmic traders.

The graphics card is essentially an expansion card that's responsible for rendering an image onto your monitor. Therefore, the better the graphics card, the better and smoother the image will be.

A great graphics card will help a trading computer run more smoothly and help you keep track of numerous graphs, charts, and tables when doing research on a specific financial instrument or when trying to read market trends.

In most cases, I'd recommend you invest in two monitors since it makes keeping track of news feeds and market trends much easier. Having a great graphics card makes this much easier and gives you a crisp display (Solanki, 2020).

RAM

RAM, random access memory, is a key component of any PC system. RAM stores the information that's actively being used by the computer so that it can be easily and quickly accessed. RAM is short-term memory.

In essence, the speed and performance of your PC are directly related to how much RAM you have installed. The more RAM you have, the faster and more efficient your PC will be.

Having enough RAM is critical when building or buying a trading computer to ensure that it's able to function properly (Samuelsson, 2019). The amount of RAM you'll need will depend on how spec-intensive the software and apps you'll be using will be.

As a general rule of thumb, a basic trading computer needs around 8GB of RAM; however, we would recommend that you aim a bit higher, for around 16 to 32GB.

The Hard Drive

The hard drive, also known as the hard disk drive, is an internally installed component that stores all your videos, documents, applications, your operating system, and pictures. In many ways, the hard drive can be thought of as a storage box. It holds pretty much everything.

Having a large hard drive isn't considered particularly important when building a trading PC. While the hard drive's main purpose is to act as a storage vault, it also has a huge impact on how quickly your PC boots up and how quickly applications and software are able to load.

Because of this, having a good hard drive is something you should seriously consider when purchasing or building a trading computer.

There are two kinds of hard drives. The first is the general HDD (hard disk drive) which nearly every computer comes equipped with. The second is the fancier SSD (solid-state drive).

When investing in a trading PC, we would recommend you go for an SSD drive instead of the more common HDD drive. This is because the SSD drive has been proven to be much faster than the HDD and will cut your boot and loading times in half.

However, SSD drives are a bit pricier than HDD drives, and if you're unable to afford it, we would suggest going with a really good HDD. It'll serve the same purpose but might be a bit slower.

Cooling

Given that a trading PC often runs at maximum capacity for extended periods of time, having an effective cooling system in place is essential to prevent overheating.

Running at max capacity for a long time will cause your PC to generate large amounts of heat and, in order to avoid overheating, the PC will forcibly slow down (Samuelsson, 2021).

To prevent this from happening, most PCs come fitted with air coolers. However, depending on the quality of the PC, these air coolers can be incredibly noisy when performing at max capacity and usually aren't able to cool the PC down enough to be very effective.

We would advise that you upgrade your cooling system by either adding better fans or installing liquid coolers. Liquid coolers are much more efficient than air coolers and are much quieter as well. However, keep in mind that liquid coolers are also much more expensive than air coolers.

The Internet Connection

Having a great, fast, and secure internet connection is essential to any kind of trade. Your internet connection is your link to financial markets and your broker platform. It is, in essence, your gateway to trades and investments.

If you want to ensure that your algorithm operates the way it should, you need a reliable internet connection.

We would recommend that you invest in some kind of backup just in case your internet fails. This could be an extra modem or even your smartphone hotspot. While not the most elegant solution, being able to connect your PC to your smartphone's hotspot can help you close any open positions and prevent you from incurring unnecessary losses.

The Minimum and Recommended Specifications for a Trading PC

Minimum Requirements		Recommended Requirements	
CPU	CPU with 4 cores	CPU	CPU with 8 cores
RAM	8GB	RAM	16GB
Storage	240GB SSD	Storage	240GB SSD

Software Requirements

Much like with the hardware requirements, you have the option of either building or programming or buying the software you'll need for algorithmic trading.

Buying ready-made software is quick and easy. However, they're not without their downsides. While buying your trading software might save you time, they won't save you money. Algorithmic software is often incredibly costly, and it might also be filled with flaws that, if ignored, could lead to unnecessary losses (Seth, 2021b).

The high costs of the software might also cut into the viability of your algorithm trading, so that's something to keep in mind.

On the other hand, building your own software allows you to customize it to your needs and offers you great flexibility (Seth, 2021b). It also doesn't cost nearly as much as buying software. However, building your own software will require time, tremendous effort, and deep knowledge of programming and how financial markets and trading work.

Key Components Every Algorithmic Trading Software Should Have

No matter if you decide to buy or build, there are a few key components that every algorithmic trading software needs in order to be viable.

Connectivity to Various Financial Markets

The most important component to any trading software is that it should have access to and be able to connect to various financial markets. This should be at both a national and international scope.

As a trader, you'll be working across multiple market exchanges. Each market will grant you access to various data feeds, and these data feeds are likely to differ in format. The software you buy or build will need to be able to accept feeds in different formats (Seth, 2021b).

If this proves too much of a challenge, you could try going with third-party data vendors, such as Reuters and Bloomberg. These data vendors provide you with aggregate market data obtained from various market exchanges. The data is also offered in a single, uniform format.

The key here is to make sure that your software should be able to process this data as required.

Backtesting with Historical Data

Another key feature that every trading software should have is the ability to conduct backtesting simulations on historical data sets. As previously discussed, backtesting involves imposing a trading strategy on historical data in order to simulate live trade, done with the aim of testing out a trading strategy in order to gauge its viability in live trading.

Backtesting is a mandatory feature; don't overlook its importance and value.

The Availability of Company and Market Data

Trading software also needs to have easy access to real-time market data feeds and company feeds. This function should be built into the system, and it should be able to easily integrate and process this information from various sources (Seth, 2021b).

Real-time data feeds contain important information like company fundamentals, company earnings, and P/E ratios. This information is essential for any trader and investor.

Latency

Latency is a time-delayed response to the movement of data points from one application to another (Seth, 2021b). For example, it might take 0.3 seconds for a price quote to register from one exchange to your software's data center (DC), it might then take 0.2 for the information to travel from your data center to your screen, and 0.3 seconds for your software to process the information.

It could then take another 0.2 seconds for your algorithm to analyze this information and place a trade, 0.4 seconds for the trade to reach the broker, and 0.3 seconds for the trade to be executed.

Given how quickly price point movements occur on the market exchange, it is likely that, within the few seconds it takes to execute a trade, the price of that asset would've changed multiple times.

In order to avoid delay and trade on the price point you want, it's important to keep the latency time as low as possible and, ideally, reduce it to microseconds. You can do this by having a direct connection to the exchange, which eliminates the need for a vendor (the middle man).

Programming that is Independent of the Platform

While it's not a requirement, having programming that's independent of the platform and software you're using is a good idea for long-term planning.

Generally, programming languages have dedicated platforms that work specifically for that software or platform. Whether you decide to build or buy, it's advised that you choose a programming language that differs from the one used by the platform you're going with.

The idea here is to prepare for any future changes that your trading strategy and algorithm might take.

Customization

Another important component of trading software is being able to customize it to suit your needs and trading strategy.

If you choose to buy, most algorithmic trading software comes with built-in algorithms. This potentially saves you time and effort; however, you should be able to completely customize the parameters of the algorithm to fit your own trade strategy.

If you buy the wrong software, you might find yourself being constrained by fixed functionality that you're unable to change.

In addition to this, being able to write your own custom programs within the software is another key feature you need to look for. This allows you to further customize and experiment with various strategies and trading concepts (Seth, 2021b).

Ideally, you should go with trading software that allows you to use your preferred programming language.

Choosing a Trading Platform

Now that you have your software and algorithm ready and hopefully tested, it's time to decide on a trading platform. But what is a trading platform? Why do you need it?

In simple terms, a trading platform is an online website or application where traders and investors are able to conduct trade and investments. Numerous online and discount brokers offer their own trading platforms either for free or at low rates, depending on the account type you hold and the broker you've chosen.

Generally, trading platforms also offer a plethora of additional services such as real-time data feeds, charting software, and premium analysis (*Trading Platform*, 2021). These services are aimed at making trade and investment as easy and as effective as possible.

There are two kinds of trading platforms: the first and most common are commercial websites, and the second are prop platforms. Commercial websites are aimed toward investors and day traders (*Trading Platform*, 2021). These kinds of trading platforms are generally easy to use and come with a vast selection of features such as educational resources, research data, news feeds, and maps.

On the other hand, prop platforms are customizable platforms developed by large brokers specifically to match their needs, style of trading, and demands.

Currently, there are hundreds of trading platforms, and deciding on which one to go with can get quite overwhelming, especially for beginners. As a general rule of thumb, you should choose a trading platform based on your trading style, trading strategy, and your financial and trading goals. You should also choose a trading platform that works well with an algorithmic trading method.

Here are a few additional factors that you should consider when choosing a trading platform:

Asset Classes

Before choosing a trading platform, you should ensure that the platform you're going for offers the asset classes that you've decided to trade. This could be stocks, bonds, etc.

Therefore, if you want to trade stocks, don't go for a platform that only supports equities. Most trading platforms support more than one asset class, which is great. Often, online brokers will offer special perks and discounts for certain asset classes. We would advise that you go for a trading platform that not only supports the asset classes of your choice but also offers perks and discounts for your chosen asset classes.

Data

As with everything in trading and investing, having access to up-to-date, relevant data is essential. The trading platform you choose should offer access to extensive, high-quality data. Some trading platforms might charge a fee for access to this information.

Ideally, you'll be able to find a trading platform that offers access to their data for free.

Broker Integration

Being able to link your algorithm to a trading platform is essential to algorithmic trading.

Unfortunately, not all algorithmic trading platforms will let you trade through them. It generally depends on whether or not the trading platform provider is a broker. If the platform provider isn't a broker, the chances are that they will allow broker integration and allow you to link your algorithm to the platform.

There are also a few platforms that don't offer any live trading support at all; this means that you won't be able to trade through them. With these kinds of platforms, all you can use them for is research and development.

It goes without saying that you should go for a trading platform that supports broker integration and allows you to link your algorithm to the platform.

Intellectual Property

A key concern for any algorithmic trader is being able to maintain the intellectual property (ownership) of the algorithms they've developed. Therefore, it's very important to find a trading platform that doesn't claim ownership rights to your algorithm if it's developed on their platform.

If this is something you're especially concerned about, we would advise you to go with a platform that lets you develop your algorithm on your own computer and then link it to the platform. This is by far the safest way to maintain your ownership rights.

Competitions and Licensing

These days, most platforms host competitions quite regularly. In these competitions, you can submit your algorithm (if it meets specific requirements) and battle it out against a ton of other algorithms (Louis, 2020).

If your algorithm wins, you could get all kinds of fun prizes or cash rewards.

Trading platforms could also offer algorithm traders the opportunity to license their algorithms and have them become officially recognized algorithms.

While these perks aren't necessarily essential to the viability and success of your algorithm trading venture, they are nice additions.

Programming Languages

Ensuring that the programming language of the trading platform supports the language you've used to develop your algorithm is essential if you want to be able to link your algorithm to the platform (Louis, 2020).

Even so, you'll still be required to learn the platform's API if you want to develop your algorithm on their platform. However, this shouldn't be much of an issue if you choose a platform that allows you to develop an algorithm on your own computer instead of on the platform.

The Knowledge Requirements

As you might have gathered by now, algorithmic trading requires more than just a fancy trading computer and access to a great trading platform. If you want to be a successful algorithmic trader, there are quite a few skills you'll need to pick up.

The first skill you'll need to learn is the **basics of trading**. This includes things like being able to read market trends, knowing what a stop order is, knowing what a limit order is, and understanding margin requirements.

There's much more to trading than just that. You'll need to know when to execute trades, when to buy and sell, and how to make the market work for you.

With the increasing popularity of trading and investing, there are numerous resources available. Many trading brokers also offer educational resources such as webinars, tutorials, and paper-trading accounts that are ideal for beginners.

If you're anything like us, you learn best by doing, and so we'd recommend you go for a paper trading account.

We'd also recommend you read more books on trading, like this one, especially those focused on the aspects of trade that interest you most. There are also numerous videos on trading and investing that you could check out online.

The key takeaway here is to learn as much as you can before moving on to live trading.

A second important skill, and something you probably weren't expecting, is **math**. Yes, we said it, if you want to be good at algorithmic trading, you need to be good at math. This entails having a good understanding of financial calculations, basic statistics, and computer trading performance metrics (Davey, 2019).

You'll also want to have a working knowledge of Microsoft Excel or some other data manipulation program such as MatLab. These programs are quite useful when supplementing your trading strategy analysis.

As much as it pains us to say, the better you are at math, the better you'll be as an algorithmic trader.

The last skill you'll need to succeed in algorithmic trading is **knowing how to run the trading platform you've chosen**. Now, this skill isn't too hard to learn.

All it takes is fiddling around with the platform a little and getting used to the mechanisms.

The best way to get acquainted with a trading platform is to open a paper trading account. This allows you to try out the platform and get used to it without committing. Closely related to this skill is being able to **follow an established scientific approach** and **learning how to develop a trading system**.

Being able to develop a sound trading system is important for designing and testing your algorithmic strategies (Davey, 2019).

The last, and probably most important skill that you'll need to learn, is **programming**. A key part of developing your own algorithm is knowing how to program and knowing which programming language will best suit your needs.

Knowing how to program is also valuable when choosing a trading software since it'll help you understand how the different software operate and which will work best for you. In addition to this, you might want to learn various programming languages as well because different platforms require different programming abilities.

The key here is to do your research and become proficient in whatever programming language is required by the trading platform (Davey, 2019).

Tips for Beginners in Programming

Approaching programming as a newbie can be quite scary. There are so many programming languages around that it can feel overwhelming. But, if you stick with it, programming can be incredibly fun and stimulating.

It's a skill that has thousands of applications. You can use your skill to create algorithms, video games, and new software. The possibilities are truly endless.

But let's reel it in a bit. In this section, I'll be giving you a few tips on how to start in programming as a beginner, with a specific focus on finance and algorithmic trading.

Google is Your Friend

Our first tip is don't be afraid to use Google. As a newbie programmer, chances are you'll make mistakes, stumble around, and get stuck trying to make codes work. If you ever feel stuck and helpless, ask Google.

There are tons of helpful videos and programming forums online; it's just a simple search away. Programming forums and tutorials are fantastic resources that you can use to improve both your skill and confidence with programming.

If you're struggling with certain commands, Google the solution. There's nothing wrong with finding answers instead of struggling your way through it. Don't be afraid to use the resources available to you.

And besides, Google is completely free, so you might as well use it.

Give it Time

This might go without saying, but give yourself time. Programming is a difficult skill to pick up, and you won't become an expert overnight. We recommend that you give yourself the time and space to fail and learn.

Think of it as a marathon rather than a sprint.

The key takeaway here is to jump in and just start. Half the battle is showing up.

Explore as Much as You Can

As we've said, programming can be intimidating. When starting out, you might try to stick to the rules and conventions as much as possible. Now, this isn't a bad thing. Following conventions is how you familiarize yourself with a new craft.

However, don't be afraid to think for yourself and try new things.

If there's a specific coding task you'd like to complete, think about how you'd like to do it. What are the steps you'd like to follow when coding? Think about the steps that are required and how you'd like to do them.

This allows you to use your creativity, and who knows, you might come up with new and exciting ways to solve problems.

Don't be Afraid to use the Print Command in R

If you're feeling intimidated by long strings of complex code and find yourself stuck on figuring out how the code works and what it does, don't be afraid to use the print command.

By simply copying the code in R, you can use the print command to help you understand how the code works and what its key functions are.

You can also use the Ctrl+Enter combination to see the code line-by-line and see the results of the console.

Chapter 3:
Getting Started with Algorithmic Trading

So, you've picked up the skills you need, you've bought or built a trading computer, and you've developed your own algorithm. What comes next?

At this point in your journey, we would assume that you've backtested and stress-tested your algorithm, and you've decided on your trading software and trading platforms. You're ready and jump in and get going.

It's all systems go!

We hate to be the party pooper, but, at this point, we would urge you to slow down.

Caution: slow down and really think about what the next couple of steps are going to look like.

In this chapter, we'll be discussing the steps you'll need to take to start algorithmic trading. We'll be taking a deep dive into how to develop your own algorithm, and we'll be providing an example of an algorithm used for trading.

But before we get to that, we'll also be going over the important things you'll need to consider before jumping in.

In many ways, this little pitstop is the point of no return. After this, you'll be fully immersed in the world of trading, and you wouldn't want all your hard work and efforts to go to waste.

Key Considerations Before Starting

Right now, you're standing on the precipice of change. Depending on where your head's at, this might be the moment before you become a fully-fledged trader, or it could be the moment you decide that this just isn't for you.

You might decide to plunge forward or turn around.

However, before you make that decision, here are a few things you should consider.

Algo Trading is Time-Consuming

Algorithmic trading is, by nature, automated trading, and this might leave you with the impression that you won't have to do much besides setting up the PC, let the algorithm run, and then rake in cash.

Unfortunately, this is hardly the case.

While the algorithm is able to run on its own, it needs human intervention and monitoring. You'll need to take time to reevaluate and reprogram your algorithm to suit shifting market trends.

You'll also need to closely monitor your algorithm to ensure that it's functioning the way you intended it to and that there aren't any flaws or oversights that could cause unnecessary loss.

You'll also need to adjust your algorithm if you decide to try out a different trading strategy.

Trading Requires Capital

Trades and investments require capital, and algorithmic trading is no different. If you want to start trading and investing, you're going to need money.

The amount you'll need to get started will vary depending on the financial market and financial instrument you choose. If you're aiming to day trade stocks, you'll need at least $25,000. Trading Forex and Futures might require less capital.

There are also costs involved with opening an account with an online or discount broker. With brokers, there are often account minimums, commission fees, and transaction fees attached to the services they provide. The trading costs will vary from broker to broker. We would advise that you carefully check out the fees structure of the broker you choose in order to avoid incurring hidden fees.

You'll probably also spend a considerable amount on purchasing or buying a trading PC and getting a hold of the various software that you'll need in order to begin algorithmic trading.

Finally, depending on whether you're a programmer or a complete newbie, you might also spend money on coding and programming courses in order to build your skill.

Goals and Objectives

Before you begin, you need to have firm, clear answers to three questions:

1. What are your financial goals?

2. What financial asset do you want to trade?

3. How much time can you commit to trading?

The key here is to have solid goals and objectives that will help you create your algorithm and decide on a solid trading strategy. Remember, you want your algorithm to work for you and help you achieve your goals.

Knowing exactly what you want and how you want to trade also helps you create your algorithm. After all, the algorithm is merely a set of instructions on how to trade. In order to code those instructions, you need to have a clear idea of your trading strategy and how to implement it.

Developing a Trading Algorithm

Developing a trading algorithm is nothing to scoff at, as you can probably tell from the long list of requirements we mentioned in Chapter 2.

An effective trading algorithm must be able to identify trade (buy and sell) opportunities and be able to execute trades according to a predetermined trading strategy. The trick is being able to convert your chosen trading strategy into lines of code that will form the trading algorithm. This algorithm will also need to be programmed to be able to access trading accounts in order to execute trades effectively.

So, how do you start?

Developing an Effective Strategy

Now, we know we've mentioned this before, and you're probably a bit sick of hearing it, but it bears repeating.

You need an effective trading strategy and, while you might have one, have you thought about how easy your trading strategy would be to code?

As a general rule of thumb, the more subjective and complex your trading strategy is, the harder it'll be to code. On the other hand, the more rule-based, structured, and simple your trading strategy is, the easier it'll be to code (Mitchell, 2021).

In general, rule-based strategies are much easier to code because they're often structured around simple instructions such as stop losses and price targets that are based on quantifiable data or price point movements (Mitchell, 2021).

These kinds of strategies are also easily copied and tested. If you're not totally comfortable coming up with your own trading strategy, there are many available online.

A resource that you could explore is Quantapedia. This website gives you access to a plethora of academic papers on trading and trading results for numerous quantitative trading methods.

No matter what your skill level is in both trading and

programming, we would recommend that you go with a rule-based trading strategy. Algorithmic trading is complicated enough as it is without making things harder by trying to code a complex trading strategy.

After all, coding takes time, and it needs to be tested and retested multiple times in order to work out all the kinks and bugs. Choosing a rule-based strategy will just aid in making your experience easier. In our knowledge and experience, the simpler the strategy, the more effective it is.

Characteristics of a Sound Trading Strategy

When choosing a trading strategy, it's important to be sure about what you would want it to accomplish. Often, it's easier to go for the easiest solution, and while that isn't necessarily a bad idea, we would recommend you do a bit more research.

Read trading blogs and forums. Check out academic finance journals and trading magazines. Basically, explore the world of trading and finance as much as you can.

Your preliminary research should be based on your personal characteristics, such as your risk profile, the amount of time you'll be able to commit, and the amount of capital you're able to set aside for trades.

That being said, here are a few key characteristics that every effective trading strategy should be:

1. Prudent of market changes
2. Based on reputable statistical methods
3. Rule-based

It should also have:

1. Clearly defined rules on when to enter, when to exit, and when to execute a trade.

2. Great portfolio management

3. Risk management

4. Make provisions for the unexpected

Figure Out What Information Your Algorithm Should Capture:

The next step is to clearly define what information your algorithm needs to capture and identify. Now, this shouldn't be too hard to figure out since it should be a key part of your trading strategy.

The aim here is to help your algorithm take advantage of market trends and behaviors (Johnston, 2021). In addition to this, we would also advise against building your strategy around one-time market inefficiencies because market inefficiencies are unidentifiable. There really would be no way of knowing whether the success or failure of your strategy happened by accident.

Now, depending on the trading strategy you choose, there are various methods that take advantage of certain market trends and behaviors. Strategies can take advantage of:

- Macroeconomic news such as interest rate changes

- Fundamental analysis such as revenue data or earnings release notes

- Technical analysis information like moving averages

- Microstructure news like trade infrastructure

- Statistical analysis such as co-integration

Now, these sources of information each contain various technical indicators that you could use in your trading algorithm. Once you become proficient at coding and trading, you could have your algorithm focus on a combination of indicators, depending on how much your trading strategy evolves.

A few popular technical indicators include:

- Moving averages

- Stochastics

- Relative strength index

- Parabolic SAR

- Relative vigor index

Once your algorithm is able to effectively and accurately capture information and process it, it'll be able to use this information (in combination with the instructions) to buy and sell financial assets and successfully execute trades.

The technical indicators mentioned are important for setting rules because, depending on their values, they'll be the trigger for your algorithm to buy or sell an asset.

You'll also need to get benchmarks to compare your strategy against!

Translate Your Trading Strategy into Code

Here's where the real fun (and the real headache) starts!

As we've mentioned before, before you're able to turn your strategy into code, there are a few key skills you'll need to pick up. Thus far, we've discussed understanding the basics of programming and having a working knowledge of trading and financial market exchanges.

In addition to this, you'll need to understand technical, fundamental, and sentimental analysis, and the inputs, variables, and math features that come along with coding.

Technical, Fundamental, and Sentimental Analysis

Having a good understanding of technical, fundamental, and sentimental analysis will help you create your code because you'll be able to understand how the indicators mentioned above work and what they mean.

But, what is technical, fundamental, and sentimental analysis?

Well, **technical analysis** is the belief that past market trends and behaviors have a direct influence over future market trends, movements, and behaviors (*Fundamental, Technical and Sentiment Analysis*, 2018).

Technical analysis traders thus rely heavily on historical data such as trend and chart analysis in order to predict potential price fluctuations and market trends. These charts generally represent price point movements over a certain period of time. By reading and analyzing these charts, traders aim to figure out future supply and demand trends of specific financial assets.

Key indicators for whether to buy or sell are the support and resistance levels. Other indicators include oscillators, trends, and volume indicators. These help traders figure out price trends.

Sentimental Analysis is more short-term than technical analysis and is focused on the sentiments (actions) of traders in general. For example, a technical analyst might predict that a financial asset is going to experience upward growth. However, the asset might remain down due to the mood of the traders.

This means that a large majority of traders have chosen a down position for some unknown reason.

These trader sentiments can be used to help traders take a particular position. Traders that follow sentimental analysis are also known as contrarians because they often invest against the trend. This is done with the belief that the market always tends to go against sentiments.

Fundamental analysis is all about studying the factors that could have an effect on the price of a financial asset. This kind of analysis is heavily dependent on the central bank of each country and the expected interest rates that they release.

It's believed that interest rate hikes can increase the value of an asset long-term. Additional factors that fundamental analysts focus on are the GDP, inflation rates, NFP releases, and population growth. Therefore, keeping up with current news is vital to a fundamental trader.

This kind of analysis is generally used in forex and commodity trading.

When creating an algorithm, understanding these analyses are vital to be able to use the technical indicators above.

Inputs, Variables, and Mathematics Features

Much like the fundamental, technical, and sentimental analyzes mentioned above, inputs, variables, and mathematical features are important when developing an algorithm.

Inputs are generally assigned to other 'nodes' in order to create an algorithm. There are four kinds of inputs that you should be aware of:

- String
- Integer
- Boolean
- Number

The **variables** generally correspond to each data type. There are four data types that you should concern yourself with:

1. Boolean

2. Text

3. Number

4. Date time

Variables are important because they'll tell your algorithm what to do and when to do it.

The **mathematical features** are pretty straightforward. These are the =, +, and - signs, to name a few.

The final aspect you should focus on is **logic,** and we don't mean common sense. Logic includes **AND**, and **Or**. For example, the algorithm could be directed to open a buy trade when the Stochastics is at 28 AND/OR when the RSI value is 30. In this case, you can use both.

In simple terms, the logic function can be used when instructing the algorithm on when to enter and exit positions.

Coding an Algorithmic Trading Strategy

Converting your trading strategy into code is where the fun begins. In our experience, this was where we were able to be the most creative. Figuring out how to translate our strategy to code was a mental exercise we didn't know we needed.

It became a game. How quickly could we code a strategy, or could we turn a complex rule into a simple code? How simple could we make the code without compromising effectiveness?

It's pretty obvious that coding is our favorite part of algorithmic trading.

In this section, we'll give you a simple 8-step method to getting your trading strategy up and running!

For this example, we'll be trading Amazon stock CFD using a simple trading algorithm. The strategy we'll be using involves buying the 'dip in prices.' What this means is that the algorithm will enter long trades when the stocks fall in value in the short term.

Here are the steps:

1. **Choose your product/financial asset.**

   In this example, we've chosen to work with Amazon stock CFD. CFD means contract for difference, and it's essentially a derivative that mimics the price point movements of the actual stock.

2. **Choose your preferred trading software.**

   Depending on how complex the software you've chosen is to install and how much RAM you have, this shouldn't take too much time.

   The software we'll be using for this example is MetaTrader 4 (MT4). We chose this software because it's super beginner-friendly, which makes it easier to use. The learning curve is also pretty flat, so if you decide to go with this software, it shouldn't take you too long to get the hang of it.

The one downside we noticed was that this software isn't great for running complex statistical analysis or machine learning. While we don't think this is something that you should worry about in the early stages of developing your first algorithm, it is something you should keep in mind.

Now, once you've downloaded your preferred software, all you have to do is open the installer and follow the instructions.

3. **Open an account with your preferred broker.**

   Once you've successfully installed your software, go to the website of your preferred online or discount broker and set up a demo account.

   Now, this may be an issue if your preferred broker doesn't offer demo accounts. If this is the case, we'd recommend you go with the next best broker that does offer demo accounts.

   The point here is to get your algorithm up and running to see if it works effectively. Think of this as a test run before the real deal. Therefore, you won't need an actual account for your first run-through.

   Depending on the broker you choose, you might need to input certain personal details. This might feel a bit risky. However, if you've done your due diligence and have chosen a reputable and respected broker, you'll have nothing to worry about.

Depending on the types of Demo accounts available, you might get to choose between a standard or premium account. Since we're just doing a test run, we recommend that you go with the standard account.

Now that you've set up your demo account, you should be given your login details.

Next, you'll want to open your trading software and find the tab that says "Login to Trade Account." With MT4, this function is under the "File" tab.

Click on this function and enter your new account details.

4. **Understand the strategy.**

As mentioned above, in this example, we'll be using a strategy that aims to buy stock once the stock dips. However, the algorithm isn't going to understand what we mean if we just type in "Buy stock when it dips."

So, in this case, we'll have to figure out what a dip means. How much does the stock have to drop to have dipped, and what duration of time should it have 'dipped' for?

It might sound like we're unnecessarily complicating things, but these are aspects you'll need to be clear on before you begin to code.

For this example, let's say that the algorithm will enter a trade when the price of the stock drops lower than its lowest price in the last 15 trading days.

Why 15 days? It really doesn't matter. You'll be able to refine this time frame during backtesting and optimization to get a number that works for you.

Now, with this exercise, we'll be going with the method of spending all the money in the account in order to buy up the max amount of shares possible each time we're able to trade.

Keep in mind that this is a very aggressive approach, and we really don't recommend it for live trading, but since our demo account gives us a bunch of fake money, let's go wild!

At this point, we'll only hold one trade at a time.

When closing the trade, we've programmed the algorithm to exit (sell) once the stock price moves up by 25% (a profit) or if the price moves down by 10% (a loss).

For example, if we enter the trade at a price point of $200, we would close the trade at either $250, making a $50 profit, or $180, thus making a loss of $20.

5. **Understand and set up your trading software.**

   Because this trading strategy is so simple and essentially governed by two fundamental rules, we won't need to use every aspect or feature of MT4.

   Generally, the more complex your strategy is, the more aspects you might need to use. However, the features you'll make use of will depend on the information you need to analyze.

   For this example, we'll be focusing on three features; namely, increasing the chart size, collecting the price data of the stock, and downloading the robot template into the trading software.

   Again, depending on your strategy, these steps will change. In addition, depending on your software, the steps to be able to do this will change.

   Once you've done this, you'll need to understand the parts of your software trading algorithm.

   Aspects that you should understand include what programming language you'll need to code in.

6. **Code your strategy.**

   Unfortunately, it would take way too long to go through an algorithmic trading code line by line, and so,we'll just be going over the basics.

That being said, there are numerous online coding courses that you can take in order to get a more in-depth explanation of coding.

Now, code is read and runs, from top to bottom.

For this trading strategy, the structure of our code would be:

Ask if the price of the stock is lower than the lowest price in the last 15 trading days

Ask price of stock < lowest price in the last 15 trading days (replace lower than with the < symbol)

Ask < lowest price in the last 15 trading days (replace ask price of stock with Ask)

Then we'll have *Ask < iLow(Symbol(), 0, (the data point contains the lowest price in the last 15 trading days))* // iLow() is a function that will give me the low price of a particular data point.

The first input will be the asset that we're working with. The second will be the time frame which is represented by 0. The third is the data point ID that we'll get for the low price.

The code would then be *Ask < iLow(Symbol(), 0, (iLowest(Symbol(), 0, MODE_LOW, 15, 1))) // iLowest()*

Now, the leap from iLow() and iLowest() can seem strange. After all, how are you supposed to know that you should code that?

The simple answer is that you wouldn't know.

When you start learning a new programming language, knowing what code to substitute for certain instructions can be tricky. That's okay. You don't need to know everything at once. If you don't know, Google it! Consult the coding forums.

Now, once your code is complete, all you need to do is compile it. When compiling a code, the program checks the code for any errors and creates a version of the code that your computer is able to understand.

7. **Run a historical test with your code.**

If your code comes back error-free, it's time to run tests!

The trading software you have installed should have a *Strategy Tester* function.

Side note: when completing these steps, we really advise that you try to find an in-depth, step-by-step video guide and follow along. Make sure that the video is using the safe software as you are. In our experience, we find learning by doing easier than just reading instructions from a page.

Once you have the Strategy Tester up and running, you can set the earliest date as your start date. Remember, you'll be using historical data to run the test!

And, just like that, the first backtest has been completed! Well done! Have a chocolate bar!

At this point, you can check the Report function to see how your algorithm did.

8. **Run it live with fake money.**

Running the algorithm live on the demo account is probably one of our favorite parts of testing code since it'll give you the best idea of whether your algorithm will work or not.

Depending on which broker you've decided to go with, you should have around $100,000 to $200,000 of virtual money to mess around with. Again, this money isn't real, so don't worry about losing it.

The first thing you want to do is open the Terminal Tab and check how much "cash" you have. Once you've done this, run the algorithm by clicking the Enable Automated Trading function.

Then, you'll want to attach the stock price chart to the algorithm (this is key information that your algorithm will need to process in order to execute trades).

And that's it! You're live!

All that's left to do is let it run and see how well you do.

Backtesting and Optimization

Depending on how well your algorithm does during the 'live testing,' you might want to revisit the code and work out any kinks and bugs.

During backtesting and optimization, you need to ensure that your code is operating exactly the way you want it to. During this time, you might also want to rethink your strategy and tweak the code so that it runs more effectively.

This could include changing the time frame, adjusting the input and variables, or fiddling with how you've coded the rules and instructions.

The aim here is to make the algorithm run as efficiently as possible.

However, a word of warning, be careful that you don't end up over-optimizing the algorithm. We've mentioned this before, but if your algorithm is too closely based on historical data, it might cause unnecessary losses since future market trends rarely follow past trends exactly.

Going Live

We know we've spoken about going live before, but that was in reference to a demo or paper trading account.

Once you've thoroughly tested your algorithm and are confident that it will work as intended, it's time to begin using real money. That's right; it's time to remove the kid gloves and start trading.

Now, as with any form of trading, there are risks involved, and this is something you'll need to keep in mind. You might also experience a few emotional ups and downs since your money will be on the line, but this is an exciting time.

Finally, you'll be able to reap the benefits of all your hard work and effort. But, before you get too excited, remember to start small. Don't put all your money into a single stock or asset.

When you're starting with live trade, take it slow and feel things out. During this time, it's also important that you constantly monitor your algorithm and market trends to see how they're performing and to check whether any adjustments are needed.

Maintenance

For as long as your algorithm is running within the statistical parameters you've instructed it to, leave the algorithm alone. While you should monitor the activity in your trading profile to ensure that it's operating correctly, don't mess with the algorithm unnecessarily.

Remember, one of the key benefits of having a trading algorithm is that human emotion doesn't hinder the trading process.

Once the algorithm is up and running, the only thing you need to do is maintain it. Monitor its performance and, if the market shifts, adjust the code accordingly.

The key here is knowing which market conditions your algorithm thrives under and which market conditions might break it down. You'll also need to understand when to leave the algorithm alone and when to intervene.

Finding a balance is tricky, and it'll take some trial and error before you're comfortable doing this. What's important is that you don't give up.

Chapter 4:
Algorithmic Trading Strategies

I've touched on algorithmic trading strategies and the importance of clearly understanding and outlining your strategy before coding in previous chapters. However, the subject of trading strategies is so important that we knew it required a chapter specifically dedicated to it.

There are a vast amount of trading strategies out there, almost as many as there are people, if not more. After all, anyone—and we do mean anyone—can develop a trading strategy completely unique to their characteristics and needs.

That being said, if we were to cover every trading strategy in every form of trade in existence, we'd be here until we were both old and gray.

So, for this chapter, we have narrowed down the field and selected the most prevalent and most popular trading strategies among algorithmic traders.

In this chapter, we'll be covering two main topics: the first is algorithmic trading strategy opportunities, and the second is algorithmic trading strategies.

If you're completely new to trading, we would suggest you pay special attention to this chapter, especially if you haven't quite figured out which strategies you'd like to try. Who knows, you might find your ideal strategy in the next few pages!

Algorithmic Trading Strategy Opportunities

So, what exactly do we mean when we say 'algorithmic trading strategy opportunities'? Well, the idea is quite simple. What we are asking ourselves (and what we think you should be asking yourself) is what opportunities are open to us if we were to begin algorithmic trading? And what opportunities lie in the strategies we could implement?

In essence, how can algorithmic trading broaden your horizons?

Well, in terms of broadening your horizons, learning how to code gives you a fancy skill to add to your resume and opens up a whole new world of possibility (Smigel, 2019). With how tech-focused our society has become, being able to code is an invaluable skill.

In addition to this, being able to write your own algorithms means that you can potentially become a pretty profitable algorithmic trader and begin earning a passive income.

In terms of algorithmic trading strategies, there are two major areas of opportunity, namely, in the strategies used and the markets that you decide to trade in (Smigel, 2019).

The biggest market opportunities that are available for algorithmic traders are to play a role in a space where institutional traders are constrained by capacity and where the data is easy to access and plentiful.

If you'd like to exploit these opportunities, we'd suggest you stay away from competitive markets like high-frequency trading.

The second opportunity is in the strategies you use. Algorithmic trading strategies generally fall into six categories.

- **Quantitative:**

  Quantitative trading strategies, as the name implies, are based on quantitative analysis. Quantitative analyses are basically mathematical computations and equations used to identify trading opportunities.

  These generally involve indicators like volume and price. A quantitative analysis then uses these indicators as inputs for the equations.

- **Mean reversion:**

  Mean reversion strategies run on the belief that the asset price volatility is temporary and will revert back to the historical mean or average price.

  Traders who use this strategy attempt to capitalize on the price of an asset once it returns to its historical average.

- **Trend-following:**

  Trend trading or trend following involves capitalizing on the perceived momentum of an asset. For example, if an asset's price is moving in a certain direction (whether up or down), it is considered a trend.

Traders might then hope to capitalize on this trend by buying as the asset is rising and then selling before the trend inevitably ends.

- **Breakout or Breakdown:**

  Breakout trading involves taking a position on an asset during the early stages of a trend. Generally, this is once an asset's price begins to rise. The aim here is to enter early and close your position once the trend begins to stagnate with the goal of generating as much profit as possible.

- **Arbitrage:**

  Arbitrage trading strategies involve simultaneously buying and selling the same asset across various markets with the aim of making a profit from the minuscule differences in the asset's listed price.

- **Rebalancing exploitation:**

  Traders who use this method aim to generate profits by capitalizing on profile rebalancing.

In addition, there are multiple execution strategies that aim to achieve the best order prices, and these are:

- Tinge-weighted average price (TWAP)
- Volume-weighted average price (VWAP)
- Percentage of volume (POV).

In this chapter, we'll be exploring each of these strategies.

Algorithmic Trading Strategies

The basis of any trading strategy is to identify an opportunity that's still profitable after taking your characteristics and financial profile into consideration. The following are popular algorithmic trading strategies.

Trend-following (Momentum-based) Strategies

Trend-following strategies, also known as momentum-based strategies, are trading strategies that aim to buy financial assets that seem to be on the rise and then selling these assets once their price has peaked (Barone, 2020).

Let's say that there's a particular trend in the market. As a trader or investor, you choose to follow this trend. In this case, traders and investors will analyze the statistical data to determine whether the trend is likely to continue.

Using this information, they'll decide when to sell the asset.

The idea is to take advantage of market volatility by finding buying opportunities that display short-term upward trends and then quickly sell once the asset has lost its momentum.

Commonly used indicators within momentum-based trading are moving averages, price point movements, and channel breakouts.

Trend-based strategies are often the easiest to code and implement via an algorithm because they don't depend on any price forecasts or predictions. The trades you make are based on the emergence of favorable market trends, and these are pretty straightforward to implement via algorithms.

Timing is vital within momentum-based trading because you need to know exactly when to buy and sell in order to avoid a loss and generate profit. This requires that you implement proper risk management techniques.

Therefore, a downside to momentum trading is that it requires proper monitoring, which could take up some of your time. In addition, if you decide to try momentum-based trading, we'd suggest you diversify your trade portfolio to safeguard against potential losses.

Now, there are two main kinds of momentum-based trading strategies. These strategies are either based on past returns or on what's called earnings surprise. Both of these aim to exploit the market reaction to various pieces of information.

- Earnings momentum strategies involve earning a profit from a market under-reaction to information linked to short-term earnings.

- Price momentum strategies involve earning a profit by exploiting the slow market responses to a larger set of information that includes the longer-term profitability of an asset.

Arbitrage Opportunities

Arbitrage opportunities involve foreign exchange and allow traders and investors to earn a profit by simultaneously buying and selling the same security, currency, or commodity across two different markets (Bloomenthal, 2019).

Essentially, the trader buys a dual-listed financial asset at a low price in one market while simultaneously selling that asset at a higher price in a different market. For example, you could buy Amazon stock at $40 in one stock market and then sell that stock in a different market (different region/country) for $100 and make a $60 profit.

It's also common for traders to exploit the arbitrage by buying and selling stock on a foreign exchange where the price hasn't yet been adjusted to the shifting exchange rate.

This method can be used for futures, options, commodities, currency pairs, and stocks.

This trading strategy is great for intermediate traders because it's very simple and should be simple to code. It's also considered low-risk, especially when compared to other trading strategies.

That being said, there are various sub-strategies within arbitrage that can be more complex. One such method focuses on keeping an eye on corporate events such as acquisition, company mergers, or the launch of a new company venture as triggers for investment and trade (Bhagat & Singh, 2018).

Traders and investors will then make moves depending on the perceived outcome of these corporate events.

Another popular method is statistical arbitrage.

Statistical Arbitrage:

Statistical Arbitrage occurs when an arbitrage opportunity emerges due to a misquote of the price point of the asset. This method can be very profitable when used in conjunction with algorithmic trading.

The aim here is to profit from the mispricing of the financial instrument based on the expected value of the financial instrument (Bhagat & Singh, 2018).

This method also works well with algorithmic trading because of how quickly you'll need to enter and exit positions due to market fluctuations. While it might be quite difficult for a human to keep up the pace and track these price point changes, an algorithm will have no such problems.

Statistical Arbitrage Algorithms are heavily based on mean revisions and work best when using the pair trading strategy. **Pair trading** is a statistical arbitrage strategy that focuses on stocks that have shown historical co-movement in prices. These stocks are pairs based on fundamental and market-based similarities.

Pair trading works with the idea that the relative prices in market exchanges exist in equilibrium and that any deviations to this rule would eventually correct themselves.

Therefore, when one stock outperforms another, it's believed that the outperformer was sold short, and the underperformer was bought long. This short-term divergence will eventually end with the prices matching up.

Let's use Pepsi and Coke as an example. Both are huge soda companies that sell pretty similar products. Historically, these companies have shared price dips and increases. Therefore, if the price of Pepsi increased significantly, while Coke stayed the same, pair traders would buy up Coke stock and sell their Pepsi stock with the assumption that the stock prices will return to their historic balance point.

If they're right, they'll earn a profit from the difference in price points from both the Pepsi and Coke stock.

While this is a pretty straightforward method, and with the right coding could lead to profit, you'll need a lot of starting capital to do arbitrage. You'll also need access to the latest technology and have the necessary expertise to make arbitrage profitable.

Index Fund Rebalancing

Before we get into index fund rebalancing, let's define what rebalancing is and how it works.

Rebalancing involves realigning a trade or investment portfolio in terms of how the assets are weighted. The purpose is to buy and sell assets in order to bring the portfolio back to the desired asset distribution.

For example, let's say your goal was to trade 20% stocks, 50% commodities, and 30% futures contracts. However, over time, you've ended up trading 50% stocks and 50% futures contracts, and your trading portfolio no longer looks the way you want it to look.

Depending on whether your trading strategy and financial aims have changed, you may decide to rebalance your portfolio so that you can reach your target allocation of 20%, 50%, 30%.

Rebalancing your portfolio also safeguards you from being exposed to unnecessary risks by ensuring that your portfolio remains sufficiently diversified and that you continue to operate within your area of expertise (Chen, 2019b).

Now, this is all good and well, but how are you supposed to make a profit from rebalancing?

Well, with index fund rebalancing, traders aim to rebalance their portfolios so that it's in line with their benchmark indices. Algorithmic traders can take advantage of this by capitalizing on the trades.

These trades could possibly offer 20 to 80 basis point profits depending on how many stocks are in the fund before it's rebalanced. Algorithmic trading works well here because the program is able to execute these trades at the correct time to ensure the best possible prices (Planning and Executing Index Rebalance Trades | Ryedale, 2021).

Quantitative-based Strategies

Quantitative trading involves trading strategies that are rooted in quantitative analysis. These kinds of trading strategies are also known as **mathematical model-based strategies** and are dependent on mathematical functions and equations to pick out trading opportunities (Sharma, 2021). When using mathematical model-based strategies, backtesting becomes vital when trying to pick out these trade opportunities.

Quantitative trading is quite innovative and exploits modern technology, the availability of data and information, and mathematics in order to trade profitably.

Generally, traders will take a trading strategy that they've resonated with and use it as the basis to create a mathematical model. Then, they'll develop an algorithm that tests this model on historical market data (Sharma, 2021).

The model will be backtested numerous times until it's been optimized to function the way the trader intends it to.

Think of it this way: let's say the weatherman processes a report and predicts an 80% chance of rain while the sun is still out. The weatherman could've come to this conclusion by collecting and analyzing climate data from the surrounding area and found that historically, this area receives rain 80 out of 100 times.

Therefore, he can state with confidence that there is an 80% chance of rain due to the results of his data analysis.

Quantitative trade strategies operate on a similar concept by using mathematical equations to analyze market data like volume, correlation to other assets, and historical price point movements in order to develop or verify a trading strategy.

A downside to quantitative trade is that your trading model has to align with financial market conditions. Therefore, there is a risk that, if the market shifts, your model might be rendered useless, and you'll have to start all over again.

Trading Range (Mean Reversion) Trading Strategies

Trading range strategies are based on the idea that price fluctuations of a financial instrument are inherently temporary and will eventually return to their average value in time (Chen, 2021).

By spotting and outlining a price range and developing an algorithm based on that price range allows trades to be executed once the price of the asset leaves this range.

The trading range strategy is often used in the statistical analysis of market conditions. This concept can also be applied to options price when describing the price volatility of an asset and how it fluctuates around a long-term average (Chen, 2021).

The best way to implement this strategy is to use it in conjunction with various forecasting techniques. The idea is that, by using these strategies and techniques simultaneously, traders will be able to spot the best possible trade opportunities.

Think of it this way: let's say when analyzing historical data, you find that the average price of a stock is $50 and that it fluctuates pretty regularly from $55 to $44. When coding this, you'll want your algorithm to have access to historical data as well as price point charts and mean average charts.

Using these inputs, you'd want your algorithm to buy stock when the price drops below $50 and sell stock once the price goes above $50, thus profiting from the price difference.

If you're well versed in reading market trends and have an effective trading algorithm in place, the mean reversion strategy could be pretty profitable. That being said, as with every strategy in trade, the mean reversion strategy is not without risk.

A major risk with this method is that you can't be 100% sure that the normal price fluctuation pattern will occur as you've predicted. Sometimes market exchanges can fluctuate unexpectedly, which could cause unforeseen highs and lows.

These events could be triggered by the release of a new product, a company merger, or the emergence of another prominent competitor.

Volume-weighted Average Price (VWAP)

Volume-weighted average price (VWAP) is a trading benchmark used by traders when trying to determine the average price of a financial asset that has been traded throughout the day. As the name suggests, the VWAP is based on the volume and price of the asset (Fernando, 2021).

Traders generally use this information to gain insight into market trends and the value of the asset.

VWAP breaks up a large order and releases the smaller chunks of the order to the market by using stock-specific historical volume profiles (Fernando, 2021). This is done with the aim to execute a trade that's as close to the VWAP as possible.

This strategy is often implemented when traders want a smoothed out indication of an asset's price over a specific period of time. It can also be used by more prominent traders when they want to ensure that their trades don't go above the price that they want to buy or sell at.

Calculating the VWAP of an asset is pretty simple. Using the VWAP, one can calculate the amount traded for every transaction and then dividing this amount by the total shares traded.

A major limitation of VWAP-based trading strategies is that VWAP is a single-day indicator. What this means is that the VWAP benchmark is restarted at the beginning of each trading day. This limits its uses, especially for algorithmic trading, because the average VWAP over a period of time is likely not accurate to the true VWAP reading (Fernando, 2021).

The VWAP is also based on historical data and, thus, is not inherently predictive.

That being said, we wouldn't recommend VWAP-based trading strategies to beginners since it can be pretty complicated to code and requires a working knowledge of market trends and financial markets.

Time-weighted Average Price (TWAP)

Time-weighted average price (TWAP) is based on the weighted average price within a particular period of time. Much like the VWAP, the TWAP is a trading algorithm that's used when traders want to execute a large number of trades.

When using the TWAP, traders are able to split a large order into numerous small orders that are valued at the TWAP price. This is done with the aim to prevent large orders from suddenly increasing the value of a financial asset in market exchanges.

Let us put it this way: executing an order for 10,000 shares will have a much larger impact on the price of those shares than, say, 100 small orders of 1,000 shares will. Larger orders, when executed, temporarily push up the value of an asset, which won't work in the trader's favor if he aims to buy.

In essence, TWAP is used to divide large orders into smaller orders in order to make trading easier for traders and investors.

TWAP can also be used by traders when they're trying to find the value of the market price of an asset. It's most commonly used by high-volume or high-frequency traders.

Calculating TWAP is pretty simple. All you need to do is average the entire day's price bar (open, high, low, and the closing prices for that day). And then, based on the time that you decided to execute the order, every day's average price is taken in order to calculate the average of the entire duration's prices.

The equation looks like this:

Average of each day's price = (Open + Close + High + Low prices) / 4

TWAP differs from the above-mentioned VWAP in that VWAP cannot be calculated as easily as TWAP. TWAP is also defined by time, whereas VWAP is defined by volume.

As simple as TWAP is to calculate, it's not without its flaws. A few downsides to this trading strategy is that it can often be too predictable, and this can leave your strategy vulnerable to other traders. This method of trade isn't sophisticated and lacks a lot of the nuances of other trading strategies mentioned in this chapter.

Percentage of Volume (POV)

The percentage of volume (POV) trading strategy, also known as the participant strategy, focuses on controlling the pace of trade execution by targeting the percentage of the market volume (*Percent of*

Volume (POV), n.d.). This is done to ensure that trade stays as close to the POV as possible.

The POV trading strategy thus aims to trade at a clearly defined percentage of the current market volume until the order set out by the trader has been completed or until the financial market closes.

When used in conjunction with algorithmic trading, your algorithm will continuously send out partial orders based on the participation/percentage ratio that you've set until the order has been completed.

So, this method of trade is most beneficial if you plan to execute high-volume trades or large orders within a specific window of time. It's also commonly used when traders are satisfied with the expected market price since POV executes trades close to market price.

Much like with TWAP, POV can also be used if traders want to limit the impact larger orders might have on the price of the asset.

Now, when implementing POV, there are a few strategy parameters you should consider. The parameters you actually end up using will depend on your trading strategy and the broker you've chosen to go with.

The first parameter you should be aware of is the start time. The **start time** determines whether or not an order will be sent to the market exchange. Therefore, you should be aware of what the start time of your market is to prevent incurring unnecessary losses. The start time will vary from financial market to financial market and from broker to broker.

The second parameter is the end time. Much like the start time, the **end time** determines whether or not an order will be executed.

The third parameter is **percentage volume**. POV, when coded into an algorithm, will automatically adjust the participation rate of your trades in order to limit the percentage of the asset's total traded volume. For example, if an asset is being traded at 100,000 shares per minute and the percentage volume is 20%, the algorithm will trade 20,000 shares a minute.

Basically, the percentage volume dictates how many shares are traded within a specific period of time.

The fourth parameter is the **price brand**. You can think of the price brand as the price limit that you can set on an asset. If the market price moves beyond the price brand limit, the algorithm won't execute the order.

The last parameter is the **reference price**. Much like the price brand, the reference price influences the price that the algorithm will execute trades at. Depending on how you've coded your algorithm, it should automatically try to beat the reference price when executing trades in order to earn larger profits.

Implementation Shortfall

Implementation shortfall is a trading strategy that focuses on the differences between the current price of an asset when a buy or sell decision is made and the final execution price after taking into consideration additional trade fees such as taxes and commissions (Hayes, 2020).

This is usually caused by a time lag between making the trade and completing it and could be due to the poor network or internet connection.

Therefore, the implementation shortfall is the sum of the execution costs and the initial (opportunity) costs should the market fluctuate between the time the order was opened and when it was closed. This is also known as a slippage.

An implementation shortfall trading strategy aims to maximize the profits earned by the trader by reducing the cost of execution. This is done by trading on real-time market exchanges. Doing this saves on not only the cost of the order but also the opportunity cost that could be incurred on a delayed execution.

Recent technological developments that have helped to minimize costs include the introduction of real-time quotes and the general move of brokers toward commission-free trading.

Additional methods you can use to minimize implementation shortfalls are using limit orders or stop-limit orders instead of market orders. Unlike market orders, a limit order will only fill at the price you want it to or a better price than the one you've set. Therefore, the order won't fill at a lower price than what you were expecting (Hayes, 2020).

A possible downside of using limit and stop-limit orders is that you might miss out on pretty lucrative opportunities. We would also advise that you only use limit and stop-limit orders when the market is favorable since they can prevent you from quickly exiting positions if the market becomes volatile.

That being said, as much as we'd like to completely eliminate this aspect of trading, implementation shortfalls are inevitable.

Sentiment-based Trading Strategies

Now, we've briefly touched on sentiment-based trading in previous chapters. In this section, we'll be doing an in-depth dive into this trading strategy and how it works.

As discussed, market sentiment is when investors or traders in general move toward or away from a particular financial instrument or market (Smith, 2019). It's a general consensus about a particular financial instrument, either a negative consensus or a positive consensus. Generally, market sentiments are positive.

Market sentiments can be seen when looking at price movements of assets. Rapidly rising prices indicate a positive market sentiment (bullish) and rapidly falling prices indicate a negative market sentiment (bearish).

Unlike the other trading strategies mentioned in this chapter, market sentiment isn't always based on fundamentals, market trends, or data and news feeds

(Smith, 2019). Oftentimes, market sentiment is driven by human emotion. It's driven by the fear of missing out on lucrative opportunities.

Technical indicators that can be used to measure market sentiment are the High-Low Index, the Bullish Percent Index (BPI), the CBOE Volatility Index (VIX), and moving averages.

Market sentiment is often used by day traders because it directly influences the technical indicators that day traders use when measuring and deciding on what to trade in order to profit from short-term price point movements.

Market sentiment can also be used by contrarian investors who aim to go against the crowd in the belief that the market will naturally correct itself once the sentiment disappears.

If they're experienced, traders and investors are also able to profit from market sentiment if they happen upon an under-or overvalued financial asset and are able to act quickly.

A major advantage of market sentiment is that you'll have to get a pretty good idea of how customers are feeling about a particular company and product. If the market has shifted toward a company, chances are they favor that company and expect it to do well. If the market has shifted away from a particular company, it's likely that they don't have much faith that the company will do well.

Market Making

A market maker (whether a firm or an individual trader) acts on both sides of the market when trading. What this means is that they provide bids and offers (asks) as well as sell financial instruments to the best offer. In this way, they're able to act on both sides of the market.

For example, let's say that a market maker is trading in Apple stocks, and they offer a quote of $20.00 - $20.05, 100x500. This means that they'll bid (buy) 100 shares for $20, and they'll offer (sell) 500 shares for $20.05, thus earning a profit from the difference between the bid price and the offer price.

Other traders and investors are then able to buy (lift the offer) the stock from the market marker at $20.05 or sell shares to them (hit the bid) for $20.

Once a market maker receives an order from another trader, they'll immediately sell shares from their holdings.

An interesting aspect about market makers is that they're somewhat shielded from the usual risks that come along with trading because they're able to offer two-way quotes in the market.

That being said, market makers still face the risk of having their securities and assets decline in value after they have been bought and before they've had a chance to sell it. After all, if the selling price is lower than the buying price, they'll make a loss.

One of the main purposes of market makers, as the name suggests, is to help make the market operate more efficiently by increasing market liquidity. They also earn a profit from the difference between the bid-ask spread.

Market makers are able to increase market liquidity by buying and selling quotations for a specific amount of assets. This can be stock, commodities, futures, or options, any financial instrument really.

In most cases, market makers are employed by larger financial firms or by the market exchange for the sole purpose of increasing the liquidity of financial markets and trade volume into financial assets.

Chapter 5:
Evaluating and Monitoring Your Algorithms

We know we've touched on the importance of monitoring and evaluating your algorithms once they're up and running. However, we have yet to give you tips on how to do so.

As we mentioned before, properly monitoring and evaluating your algorithms is an essential step for any algorithmic trader, no matter their skill and experience level.

For algorithmic traders, their success in trading is completely dependent on whether or not their algorithms are able to operate efficiently. In addition, their strategies and systems also need to be adaptable to variance since market conditions are often in flux and dependent on the underlying economic environment.

Market conditions, exchanges, and trends are also always changing and can behave in unpredictable ways. Therefore, it's important to ensure that the algorithm that you've programmed is updated to remain compatible with current market conditions and trends.

One of the key reasons to evaluate and monitor the

performance of your algorithm is to ensure that it remains up to date and doesn't become irrelevant and incompatible with the financial market that you're working in.

In this chapter, we'll be giving you a few pointers on how to check if your algorithm is still able to keep up with market trends and perform well, as well as how to know when it needs to be updated.

Evaluating Trading Strategies

Technological development and innovation have progressed in leaps and bounds in recent years, and this has been golden for algorithmic and systematic traders. Not only have these technological developments drastically changed the landscape of finance, trade, and investment, they have also made the process incredibly easy and user-friendly.

One area that has been improved is evaluating and monitoring algorithms. Current market analysis platforms have made it incredibly simple for algorithmic traders to review their trading systems.

Evaluating and monitoring your algorithm has become as simple as compiling a strategy performance report and judging whether or not the algorithm still meets your trading and financial needs.

Strategy performance reports are compiled by applying performance metrics to your algorithm and are essentially a compilation of different datasets based on various mathematical aspects of your algorithm's performance (Folger, 2019). This report is essentially an objective overview of how your algorithm has performed within the financial market exchange. Analyzing the strategy performance report of your algorithm is a great way of finding the strengths and weaknesses in your algorithm.

Think of it as a tool to help you find what's working in your algorithm and what isn't. This tool can be used when backtesting and using historical data, as well as when your algorithm goes live.

For algorithmic traders, strategy performance reports are invaluable. Most market analysis platforms offer this feature to traders, particularly during backtesting. Most online brokers should offer this feature as well, although it might be hidden behind a paywall.

Key Components of a Strategy Performance Report

When analyzing a strategy performance report, you should be familiar with the general format the report will take and how you should read it. Now, in our experience, strategy performance reports have a pretty standard format all around. However, there might be slight differences depending on which online broker or market analyst platforms you've chosen.

Some brokers and market analyst platforms might have different methods of displaying data, and it might take a few tries to get the hang of them.

That being said, there are a few basic components of a strategy performance report that you should familiarize yourself with.

Front Page (Summary)

The front page of the strategy performance report is essentially a summary of the performance metrics and the rest of the data in the report. It's a snapshot of how your algorithm has performed in the financial market over a specific period of time.

This information is commonly displayed in a table format with the performance metrics listed on the left of the table and the corresponding calculations listed to the right of the table.

Key Performance Metrics

Key performance metrics that should be listed in both the summary and within the report are the *total net profits*, the *percentage profitable*, *average trade net profit, profit factor,* and *the maximum drawdown*. As you can probably tell, these metrics are good indicators of how well your algorithm is performing.

It's very likely that your strategy performance report will contain a plethora of data, statistics, and information. However, these metrics are the most relevant when evaluating performance.

Performance metrics are usually illustrated using graphs that display the trade data of each metric over a specific period of time.

These metrics are a great starting point for beginners who are still getting the hang of analyzing data and implementing trade strategies. They're also great if you want an initial scope of the performance of your algorithm before diving into the rest of the data.

But what do these key metrics mean? Here is a quick breakdown:

1. Total Net Profits

The total net profit is essentially the bottom line or the ultimate goal of a trading system over a specific period of time. After all, the goal of trade is to generate profit, and this performance metric tells you how much net profit you've earned.

The total net profits are calculated by subtracting the gross loss of all trades (this includes any trade fees such as commissions or holding fees) from the gross profits of all successful trades. The equation should look something like this:

> Gross Profits - (Gross Loss + Trade Fees) = Total Net Profits

The total net profits metric is a great indicator of performance and the viability of both your trading strategy and your algorithm; however, it cannot be viewed in isolation. Trusting this metric alone can be quite deceptive since it isn't an accurate indicator of whether your algorithm is actually performing effectively.

This indicator is also unable to normalize the results of the algorithm when taking into consideration the amount of risk involved.

Therefore, while an invaluable metric, we would strongly advise against reading it in isolation.

2. Percentage Profitable

The percentage profitable indicates the probability of your algorithm to execute successful trades. Unlike with the previous performance metric, there isn't one ideal value that every trader should aspire to. Instead, the 'ideal value' varies from trader to trader, depending on your trade style and strategy.

When trend trading, traders will often have a lower percentage profitable value because they typically execute larger trades that involve potentially large profits. This is because successful trades generate huge profits.

When using this method of trade, the percentage profitable value can be as low as 40%, and yet, the trader might still be wildly successful due to the large gains. Trades that are unsuccessful are also usually closed at a small loss when compared to the gains.

The percentage profitable is calculated with the following equation:

(Successful Trades ÷ Total Number of Trades) x 100 = Percentage Profitable

3. Average Trade Net Profit

The average trade net profit refers to the average amount of money that you gained or lost per trade. This performance metric considers both successful and unsuccessful trades and is based on the total net profit metric discussed earlier.

A downside of this metric is that it can easily be skewed by an outlier. For example, a single trade that generated a much larger profit when compared to the others can throw off the average trade net profit. This can result in an overinflated average trade net profit value that can make you seem much more profitable than you really are.

To avoid this, you could remove the outlier from the equation for a more accurate value.

The average trade net profit is calculated as follows:

Total Net Profits ÷ Total Number of Trades = Average Trade Net Profit

4. Profit Factor

The profit factor is the gross profit divided by the gross losses (+trade fees). This metric considers all trades conducted during an entire trading period. This is done in order to find out the amount of profit you generate per unit of risk.

The profit factor is calculated as follows:

Total Gross Profits ÷ (Total Gross Losses + Trade Fees) = Profit Factor

However, unlike with the percentage profitable, there is an ideal value that you should aim for.

For example, let's say your total gross profits are $149,020, and your gross losses combined with your trading fees are around $75,215. When using the calculation, you should have a profit factor of 1.98.

Now, 1.98 is a very reasonable profit factor and is an indicator that your trading algorithm generates a profit. While risks and losses are inherent in trade, your goal should be to offset those losses and the potential risk by consistently generating a profit.

By using the profit factor, you'll know just how much your profits outweigh your losses.

If your profit factor is below 1, for example, a 0.94, this means that your gross losses exceed your gross profits, and therefore your algorithm isn't successfully generating profits. In this case, we would strongly advise that you reevaluate your algorithm and trading strategy.

5. Maximum Drawdown

The maximum drawdown is essentially the 'worst-case scenario' for a trading period (Folger, 2019). This performance metric helps traders measure the amount of risk they might sustain because of the algorithm. It also helps you figure out whether your algorithm is viable, based on how large the account is.

The basic premise here is that if the amount of cash you're willing to risk is less than the maximum drawdown, it's likely that the trading system you've come up with is not suited for you. In that case, we would advise you to go back to the drawing board and rethink your trading strategy and algorithm.

What makes the maximum drawdown such an essential metric is that it acts as something of a wake-up call, especially to idealistic and newbie traders. This metric needs to align with your risk tolerance and the size of your trading account.

There's nothing wrong with dreaming big and shooting for the stars; however, if you want to achieve your financial goals, they need to be realistic. The same goes for your trading strategy.

Additional Aspects That You Should Evaluate

While the strategy performance report is the main, and possibly the easiest method you could use when evaluating your trading strategy, it shouldn't be the only method you use.

Your strategy performance report is a great way to get a general overview of how your algorithm has been performing. However, if you want to get the full picture, you should consider the following aspects:

1. **Methodology**

   As the name implies, the methodology refers to how, why, where, and when you're implementing your strategy. This aspect focuses on the parameters of your strategy, the market conditions, broker, trading strategy, code, and so forth.

   The methodology essentially involves everything you've done up until this point.

   When evaluating your methodology, you're basically retracing your steps with the aim of finding out where you might've made mistakes. This means thinking through every step and choice you've made and deciding if they were sound or not.

   Now, this might sound like a lot, but it's very simple. When evaluating your methodology, we suggest you use your strategy performance report as a guide.

   For example, if your profit factor is low, you can focus on evaluating your trading strategy, as well as your trading fees and expenses. Oftentimes, a low-profit factor could be because you're being charged for hidden fees by your broker.

In this case, your profit factor would be directing you to specific areas of your algorithm and trade that need your attention. All you have to do is rethink your methodology in these areas and pick out the weak points.

2. Frequency

The frequency of your trading strategy refers to how often your algorithm executes trades. Therefore, high-frequency trading means that you'll be executing a lot of trades throughout a trading period, while low-frequency trading means that you're executing a small number of trades throughout a trading period.

High-frequency trading strategies are commonly used by day traders.

Now, high-frequency trading has the potential to generate large profits; however, it also carries the risk of incurring large losses. That being said, one of the things you should consider is whether you're willing to risk enough capital for the number of trades you'd like to execute.

For example, you'll need a lot of capital for high-frequency trading and less capital for low-frequency trading.

A good indicator of this is the maximum drawdown performance parameter mentioned above.

3. Parameters

The parameters of your algorithm and trading strategy are essentially the limitations of your algorithm. Therefore, your algorithm cannot perform beyond the parameters that you've set during coding.

If you refer back to Chapter 3 we discussed knowing the rules of your trading strategy and being able to code those rules. Well, the parameters are those rules. They tell your algorithm how and when to operate. They also limit how much and how often your algorithm executes trades.

If you're having trouble with your algorithm's performance, the first aspect we recommend you check is your rules.

Oftentimes your algorithm might be struggling because of the rules you've set. Perhaps you haven't thought them through properly or coded them correctly. Sometimes, the entire trading strategy is wrong, and you have to go back to the drawing board.

4. Volatility

Volatility refers to the amount of risk associated with a trading strategy. This aspect of your trading strategy and algorithm should be present in the strategy performance report.

This aspect focuses on not only your trading

strategy but also the financial asset you'll be trading.

Therefore, the higher the volatility of an underlying asset, the higher the risk of a loss. The lower the volatility, the lower the risk.

The volatility rate is often illustrated using the Sharpe ratio. The Sharpe ratio was developed by William Sharpe, hence the name, and is used to analyze and understand the return of an investment when compared to the risk (Fernando, 2019).

Generally, the larger the Sharpe ratio, the better the risk-adjustment return. Therefore, when using this calculation, it's best to aim for a higher Sharpe ratio because that would mean that the reward far outweighs the risk.

So, what happens after you've analyzed your strategy performance report? Well, we suppose that answer depends on the results of your report. If the report is favorable and your algorithm and trading strategies are working as intended, there isn't much you need to do.

At this point, you might have decided to tweak your trading strategy a bit in order to make it more effective, but other than minor changes, you should be feeling pretty confident. We know we would be.

On the other hand, if your report has worrying results, your next step is to take an in-depth look at your algorithm and strategy and try to figure out where you might've gone wrong. This could entail doing more backtesting and stress testing, going back and checking the code, or reevaluating current market conditions.

Here are a few steps you can take after evaluating your algorithm:

Determine Whether There's a Need For Change

After you've analyzed your strategy performance report and have gone over all the performance metrics and performance values, you need to determine whether there's a need for a change.

Ask yourself whether it's time to adjust your trading strategy. Is there a genuine need for change? Now, finding the answers to this question isn't that difficult.

Check your strategy performance report. The answers lie within the values you'll find there. Therefore, if the statistics and values are poor, you should probably rethink your strategy. However, if your results are great, then you could think about making a few tweaks, but there isn't much to worry about.

That being said, in our experience, having a new algorithm go live can be quite thrilling. The first time we ran an algorithm live, using real money, our stomachs were twisted for days. We were glued to our PCs, constantly checking and rechecking our algorithm.

You might experience a similar state of anxiety, and this could cause you to evaluate your strategy before your algorithm has had a chance to prove itself.

Our point here is that you have to give it time. Don't rush in with an evaluation until you've given your algorithm a chance to thrive.

As mentioned previously, your trading strategies need to be versatile and be able to operate effectively within the constantly fluctuating market conditions. However, in order to test your algorithm's viability across fluctuating market conditions, you need to give it time.

Figure Out How Much You Need to Adjust

After you've decided whether or not you actually need to adjust your algorithm, you need to figure out how extensive those adjustments need to be. Do you need slight tweaks here and there, maybe shifting a few calculations and a bit of code around, or do you need to overhaul the entire system and start from scratch?

The extent of the adjustments often depends on the performance of your algorithm. A good way to figure out which aspects of your algorithm need adjusting is by looking at your strategy performance report.

In our experience, we've found that checking out the performance metrics is a great way of figuring out where the weaknesses and errors are. In that case, you can pick apart those aspects which might be giving you trouble and make adjustments to them instead of having to overhaul the entire system.

It could also be that there's nothing inherently wrong

with your algorithm, and it could just be experiencing system death. System death is when your algorithm is no longer viable or effective within current market exchange conditions.

In this case, you'll have to carefully break apart your system and find the aspect of your algorithm that no longer serves its purpose. It could be an indicator that has changed or that certain aspects of your algorithm have become ineffective. It could also be that your algorithm lacked true versatility.

Either way, breaking apart your system and analyzing each aspect can be ridiculously time-consuming and frustrating. It's also a difficult method of going about adjusting your algorithm and requires extensive experience and knowledge regarding trade, technical indicators, and coding.

If you're forced to overhaul your algorithm and design and build a new trading system, you'll have to dedicate quite a bit of time to it as well. Overhauling a system takes much more thought, effort, and consideration than just finding and making minor adjustments.

The key point in this section is that you need to be able to pinpoint the weaknesses and strengths of your algorithm by observing your algorithm's performance and the performance metrics. Basically, you need to be able to identify what is working and why, as well as what isn't working and why.

Once you have that figured out, you need to know how extensive your adjustments need to be.

That being said, it's also important to note that fiddling with one aspect of your algorithm has a ripple effect on every other aspect of your algorithm. Therefore, when making minor adjustments, be aware of the effects it's having on the entire system. The worst-case scenario is when you adjust one aspect, and it ends up making your whole algorithm unstable.

Making The Necessary Adjustments and Live Testing

Once you've figured out the issues in your algorithm and you've made the necessary adjustments, it's time to test the system via backtesting and stress testing. Now, we've been over this before, and, once again, the best-simulated tests you can run are on demo accounts or paper trading accounts (*6 Steps to Evaluate Your Trading Strategy for Optimal Performance*, 2019).

However, you should be careful not to get caught in the paper trading phase or try to make your algorithm perfect since this could lead to over-optimization. Getting stuck in paper trading also won't benefit you much if you're trying to learn more about live market operations.

Again, don't be afraid to take your time. With trading, there really is no rush. Trading opportunities will always be available.

What's important in this step is to carefully observe your algorithm's performance metrics while testing and running simulations. It's also wise to run your algorithm through various iterations of the simulation, allowing you to objectively and comprehensively evaluate the viability and effectiveness of the adjustments you've made.

Regular Evaluations

Now, we've mentioned this before, but certain lessons bear repeating. If we lived in an ideal world, all your algorithms would run perfectly without needing intervention, and you would generate enough profit that you'd be able to live off the interest.

Unfortunately, the world is as flawed as we are, and your algorithm might be good, but it won't be perfect (*6 Steps to Evaluate Your Trading Strategy for Optimal Performance*, 2019). Therefore, it's essential that you conduct regular evaluations in order to maintain its efficiency.

If you're able to do this successfully, you should notice considerable improvements when comparing your past strategy performance reports with current and future performance reports.

That being said, it's important to ensure that when evaluating your strategy, you give your algorithm the space and time to settle within the market exchange and prove itself. Then, when evaluating your algorithm, you'll have enough data to work with.

Oftentimes, if you're too early with your evaluation, you'll have a relatively small data sample to work with, and this can cause misleading results.

Iterate

Iteration is key when monitoring and evaluating your algorithm. In fact, we'd go as far as to argue that iteration forms part of every step of developing and running an algorithm.

In short, no matter which part of the process you're in, you'll need to run your algorithm through numerous iterations until you're able to get the desired result. For example, when developing a trading strategy, you might have to test out various iterations of a trading strategy before you settle on one that suits you. When converting that strategy into code, you might also need to test out various iterations of the code before you're able to land on one that works as intended.

The point here is to test and retest and refine your strategy and algorithm until it serves your purpose.

If you're finding trouble with any of these steps, don't be afraid to ask for help. Often, our eyes miss what is very clear to others, so don't be afraid to scroll the forums. Who knows, you might even make a friend!

Monitoring Your Algorithm

When evaluating your algorithm, it's likely that you'll only conduct evaluations after a trading period, or bi-annually. In our experience, evaluations aren't that effective when conducted too frequently.

On the other hand, monitoring your algorithm should be a more frequent activity. Unlike evaluation, monitoring your algorithm doesn't have to be as time-consuming. In most cases, it could entail checking in on your trading account, your trading profile, and your algorithm just to see if it's operating the way it should.

Monitoring your algorithm is vital, especially if you're a beginner or if you're running a new algorithm. The main aim is to ensure that your algorithm is operating as intended, as well as picking up on any possible bugs, weaknesses, or errors in your algorithm.

Having easy access to your trading portfolio and trading account is a great way to monitor the progress and performance of your algorithm. This is also a great way to keep track of all the trades your algorithm is making.

These days, most online and discount brokers offer a mobile app platform that automatically syncs your trading profile and account to your cellphone. You're also able to make trades and manage your account from these apps.

Having a mobile trading app on your cell phone allows you to quickly and easily monitor the performance of your algorithm from wherever you are in the world. All you need is an internet connection.

Mobile trading apps are essential for any trader, whether you have a busy lifestyle or not. They give you the freedom to spend your time as you wish without having to be chained to your PC, executing trades, or monitoring your algorithm.

In our experience, having access to a mobile trading app also took a lot of pressure off our shoulders when we first started with algorithmic trading. It allowed us to peel ourselves from our computer and gave us the comfort of knowing that we could check on our trading profile and account whenever and wherever we wanted.

Therefore, we would advise that, when looking for an online broker, you choose one that offers a great mobile platform. It's also important to ensure that the mobile app is supported by your mobile device.

Chapter 6:
Risk Management

Up until this point, we've mentioned the risks associated with trading and the inherent risks that come along with each trade executed. In the previous chapter, we also went over a few performance metrics, a few of which covered risks when calculating the viability or profitability of trades.

However, thus far, we haven't told you how to manage risks. Notice how we didn't use the word 'avoid' because, while risks can be mitigated and managed, it's impossible to avoid them completely.

Every trade, no matter the method, asset, or strategy, comes with some measure of risk. Unfortunately, in the world of trade and finance, risks are unavoidable. Therefore, it's vital that every trader and investor implement some form of risk management strategy before proceeding.

Now, oftentimes the risk strategies one can employ when trading is inherent in the trade strategies. Think about it. In previous chapters, we've spoken extensively about evaluation, backtesting, and making use of paper trading accounts when testing out new strategies and algorithms.

These steps are essentially a form of risk management. For example, when backtesting, you're ensuring that your trading strategy and algorithm work the way you intend it to. This lessens the risk of incurring unnecessary losses because your algorithm is ineffective.

The same goes for regular monitoring and evaluations.

In this chapter, we'll discuss the risks unique to algorithmic trading, as well as trading in general, and how to manage these risks. We'll also be covering the common mistakes made by newbie traders and how to avoid them.

Risks

There are a plethora of risks associated with trade and investment. There are also different risks associated with different trading strategies and methods. Therefore, one of the first things you'll need to do when deciding on a trading strategy and method is to consider the risks involved.

For example, the risks associated with day trading might be different from the risks associated with swing trading, and high volume trading carries different risks than high-frequency trading.

That being said, there are specific risks associated with algorithmic trading that you should be aware of before you jump in.

High Volatility

As we've discussed before, in order for your algorithm to be effective, it needs to be able to handle changes in market conditions. Not only will you need to be able to anticipate certain market changes, but you'll also need to ensure that your algorithm is flexible enough to handle these changes. Now, coding your algorithm to be able to handle market-related changes is no walk in the park. It requires a good working knowledge of trading and financial market exchanges, as well as great coding skills.

Even if you're able to code a flexible algorithm that's able to handle market changes, there's always the risk that your algorithm might react adversely to market changes by excessively widening the bid-ask spread, or it may stop functioning altogether.

This could lead to increased volatility and a decrease in liquidity. In the worst-case scenario, your algorithm could continue functioning but be executing risky trades due to changing market conditions, thus increasing your losses.

Incorrect Algorithms

Another major risk that algorithmic traders face is implementing a faulty algorithm. This could be because you didn't code a specific instruction correctly, or you haven't thought through your strategy enough. It could also occur if you haven't set clearly defined rules and instructions or if you've misunderstood how a trading strategy operates.

Whatever the reason, an error or weakness in your algorithm could cause an increase in losses over a very short period of time.

While the risk exists, it can be managed by backtesting your algorithm and testing it out on paper trading accounts. However, too much backtesting can lead to over-optimization.

As discussed, over-optimization occurs when your algorithm works amazingly when backtesting yet isn't compatible with current, live market fluctuations and changes. In this case, your algorithm might seem like it works perfectly when conducting backtesting because you've unintentionally fit your algorithm to historical data and market trends instead of live market conditions.

In this case, the performance of your algorithm when backtesting is misleading and won't correlate with its performance in live market exchanges.

Chain Reactions

Global markets have become increasingly integrated due to rapid technological developments in the world of finance. Therefore, when a change occurs in one financial market, the change often ripples over to other markets and asset classes.

This causes a chain reaction.

In this case, a chain reaction could cause unexpected changes to market conditions that you might not have accounted for. Your algorithm might not be able to handle these changes, and thus, you run the risk of having to intervene and adjust your strategy to fit current market conditions.

These chain reactions can also happen quite rapidly, depending on how active the market exchanges are and how huge the shift in the market is. These changes can be triggered by external factors such as company mergers, the introduction of a new product, or a natural disaster.

System Failures

Given that the algorithm is held and run completely electronically, with very little human intervention, algorithmic traders do run the risk of having their hardware or software fail.

It could be that there's a power outage, or their trading computers simply aren't up to running the software anymore. In some cases, it could be that the computer systems become overloaded, which causes the power supply to blow.

No matter the cause, if something goes wrong with the hardware or software, the algorithm ceases to function, which could cause trades to halt and positions to be left open.

This can cause an increase in losses, especially if you're making high frequency or high volume trades.

In addition to the loss of trade, depending on the extent of the system failure, you might need to spend large amounts of money fixing what has been broken. This could include replacing key components, software, and in the worst-case scenario, having to build a new system altogether.

If this occurs, we recommend you access your trading account and halt all activity until you're able to get things back up and running. We also recommend that you keep backups of all your data, programs, codes, and algorithms in case of a system failure.

Having these backups will make it easier for you to get back on track once your system has been restored.

Network Connectivity

As much as your algorithm is dependent on your trading computer to function optimally, it's also dependent on having a strong internet connection. Now, if you live in a fairly advanced country or city, this shouldn't be much of a problem since WIFI has become almost commonplace in certain areas.

In addition to having access to a wireless internet connection, your connection also has to be strong and stable enough to conduct trades at a consistent rate.

If your network connection cuts out due to a power failure or nasty weather conditions, your algorithm won't be able to function correctly, and you could incur some unnecessary losses.

Unfortunately, ensuring you have a stable, reliable internet connection isn't always something you're able to control. There's always the risk that the connection might cut out and disrupt your trading.

Risk Management

We know why risk management is important, but what exactly does it entail? In simple terms, risk management is needed to reduce losses when trading or investing. Proper risk management can also be used to help protect trade and investment accounts from losing money.

As discussed above, risks occur when losses are incurred. Given the inherently risky nature of trade and investment, risk management is a necessary component of any trader's arsenal. With the proper risk management strategies in place, a trader or investor is able to access market exchanges without the fear that they'll lose all their cash (Kuepper, 2019).

While there are a few risk management strategies inherent in the process of developing a trading strategy and algorithm, having this as your only form of risk management isn't nearly enough if you want to trade successfully.

Now, depending on your trading strategy and trading methods, the risk management strategies you implement will vary. However, there are a few common risk management strategies that have universal appeal.

Here are a few **common risk management tips** that should work for the everyday trader:

Coming to Terms with Loss

This tip might sound completely out of the realm of possibility when discussing risk management. After all, the entire point of risk management is to avoid risks and losses as much as possible, right?

However, as we've mentioned previously, risks are inherent to trade. No matter how effective your strategy and how robust your risk management strategies are, there will always be some measure of risk. It is inevitable.

Because of this, we think it's really important to acknowledge the risks that come along with trade and investment and realize that each trade comes with risks. Sometimes things don't work out the way you want them to. Sometimes market trends end unexpectedly, or the market shifts in ways that you might not have predicted.

Therefore, acknowledging these risks help you better prepare for them, both emotionally and financially.

Risk management exists not to eliminate losses but to keep your losses small and manageable while ensuring that your gains outweigh your losses (Desai, 2016).

Entry Points

One of the key skills you'll need to develop in order to become a successful trader is knowing how to read the market and identify trade and investment opportunities. Part of this skill is knowing when to enter and exit positions in order to generate the best possible gains.

Knowing when to enter and exit positions is something many traders struggle with, no matter their experience level, so don't feel too discouraged if you stumble around a bit. The main problem with this aspect of trading is that there isn't a right or wrong way of doing it.

Trade and investment are generally wildly subjective, and strategies will vary from trader to trader. Therefore, it can be hard to pin down exactly how to go about trading.

However, there are a few general guidelines and pieces of advice that can help you figure things out.

If you find a rapidly growing stock or an asset that's increasing in momentum, as tempting as it might be to jump in and buy up a ton of stock, we would advise that you wait. Watch the asset carefully and wait for the asset to reach its stride. Once you've found a reliable pattern to the asset's increasing momentum, you can enter a position with the knowledge that you'll be able to spot your exit points.

In addition to this, we suggest you check out market indicators and use them as guidelines for entering and exiting positions.

Now, with algorithmic trading, knowing when to enter and exit positions shouldn't be too much of an issue since your algorithm would have been programmed with specific instructions on when to enter and exit positions.

That being said, you'll still need to decide when your

algorithm will enter and exit positions when developing your trading strategy and coding your algorithm.

Diversifying Your Portfolio

Diversifying your trading or investment portfolio is one of the most important aspects of trading. Essentially, this approach to trade is based on the age-old saying, 'Don't put all your eggs in one basket,' What this means is that, if you invest all your cash into one stock or financial instrument, you run the risk of experiencing massive losses if the stock or asset plummets.

To mitigate this risk, it's strongly advised that you diversify your portfolio by investing in and trading a wide variety of stocks and financial assets. That way, if one of them fails, the loss you'll experience won't be as devastating.

That being said, it's also important to make sure your portfolio is evenly balanced. Or at least that it's balanced according to your trading strategy. Having a properly balanced portfolio serves a similar purpose to diversifying your portfolio in that it mitigates some risk and increases the likelihood of generating profits.

See, it's really quite simple. A diversified portfolio consists of various stocks and financial assets and, therefore, affords you more opportunities to generate profits and decreases your risk of incurring major losses.

Hedging

Hedging is essentially a trading strategy that aims to offset any potential losses. This means trading and investing with the aim of reducing risks. This entails hedging against the market price risk in order to protect yourself against any negative price movements by obtaining a price lock (Thakar, 2020a).

A price lock kicks in when the price of an asset moves beyond a predetermined limit. Once this happens, all trades stop for the day or until the price moves back within the limit. For example, if the price of an asset drops below the limit, your algorithm can be programmed to halt all trading until the price moves above this limit.

This prevents you from making large losses if the price of an asset drops substantially.

This trade and investment strategy is often done using derivatives (a financial instrument) since the relationship between derivatives, and their corresponding underlying asset is clearly defined (Thakar, 2020a).

If you're not a fan of derivatives, this strategy also makes use of futures contracts, options, and over-the-counter stocks.

Implementing hedging when using algorithmic trading is pretty easy since you're able to code hard price locks, and your algorithm will abide by these price locks without much intervention.

The Risk/Reward Ratio

As mentioned, whenever a trader decides to enter or exit a trade, they need to consider the risks involved. The goal for every trader should be to have the "reward" (profit) outweigh the risks.

Therefore, if the risks associated with a trade are high and outweigh the reward, there's no point in entering it. On the other hand, if the risks associated with the trade are low and the reward outweighs the risk, it would be beneficial to enter the trade.

The risk to reward ratio trading strategy is often used by conservative traders who are more cautious when entering and exiting positions in order to lower their risk as much as possible.

While there's nothing wrong with conservative trading, we would caution against being overly cautious when trading. Allowing your fear of risk and losses to dictate your trading could cause you to miss out on generating profits. Luckily, algorithmic trading removes human emotion from the equation, so you shouldn't have much to worry about in that department.

The key challenge with the risk/reward ratio strategy is knowing how to balance the risk and the reward because, in trade and investment, the higher the risk, the higher the reward.

The risk/reward ratio you settle on will depend on the trading method you use (day risk-reward, high-frequency trading, etc.). For example, day traders should aim for a 1:2 risk/reward ratio. What this means is that if you make a $100 trade, you should be willing to lose $200.

The risk/reward ratio aims to give traders a clear idea of potential profits and losses related to each trade they make. This allows you to make informed decisions when trading. Implementing a risk/reward ratio will also prevent you from executing trades that could put your entire account at risk.

Regular Maintenance

Just like how you should regularly monitor and evaluate your algorithm, the same goes for your trading PC. For algorithmic traders, their trading PCs are their bread and butter. Without them, algorithmic trading would be impossible.

Therefore, it's vital to run regular maintenance checks on your hardware and software. Most PCs come with preinstalled tune-up programs that check the efficiency of your PC. Running tune-ups and service maintenance ensures that your PC is running in optimal condition and lowers the risk of system failures.

You could also use this time to evaluate the condition of your PC and its components and decide whether a hardware update is needed. Perhaps your power supply needs to be upgraded, or you'd like to invest in a better motherboard.

The point here is to ensure that your PC is able to keep up with your trading algorithm and run your trading ventures efficiently and effectively.

Scenario Analysis

Scenario analysis is another method that can be used to manage risks. This method involves estimating the anticipated value of a trade or investment portfolio after a predetermined period of time (Hayes, 2019). This is done on the assumption that the value of the assets held in the portfolio is subject to change, for example, a change in the interest rate.

Traders can implement scenario analysis to estimate the changes in value of their portfolios in response to hostile market changes or conditions. This method is also commonly used to estimate the value of portfolios in theoretical worst-case scenarios.

Scenario analysis is done by computing various reinvestment rates for anticipated returns that are reinvested. These calculations are based on mathematical and statistical principles (Hayes, 2019).

Using these calculations, scenario analysis provides some idea of how the value of your trading or investment portfolio might change in "what if" situations.

Essentially, it answers the question of how your trading portfolio will perform if the market crashes or if it shifts in a different direction.

Now, we know that some people insist that you should conduct a scenario analysis before you enter a trade, but in our opinion, this is a bit excessive. With an algorithm, you're able to set certain parameters and limitations. These limitations should be set with the potential risks in mind. If you've done this correctly, we think conducting scenario analysis before each and every trade is simply ridiculous.

We would advise that you implement scenario analysis at the beginning of your trading strategy development and coding so, once your algorithm is up and running, you don't have to waste time constantly doing scenario analysis since your algorithm will already be taking this into consideration.

Portfolio Optimization

Portfolio optimization involves building your portfolio with the aim of maximizing anticipated returns while minimizing the risks. Now, how you choose to optimize your portfolio will depend on your trading strategy and financial goals.

Portfolio optimization is based on the Modern Portfolio Theory (MPT). The MPT was pioneered by Harry Markowitz in his paper "Portfolio Selection," which was first published in 1952 in the Journal of Finance (Chen, 2019b). This is a theory on how traders can build portfolios to maximize anticipated returns based on the level of market risk associated with the portfolio. This theory also argues that the risk and return associated with an investment or trade shouldn't be viewed in isolation but instead should be evaluated in terms of how this investment affects the overall risk and return rates of the portfolio.

That being said, optimizing your portfolio essentially involves analyzing various portfolios that have different proportions of investments by calculating the potential risks and rewards (profits) that each portfolio could generate (Thakar, 2020a). This is done with the aim of finding the perfect combination of assets that will yield the maximum amount of profits with the least amount of risk.

Common Beginner Mistakes and How to Avoid Them

Now that we've gone over the common risks associated with algorithmic trading and how to mitigate those risks via risk management strategies, we thought it would be helpful to cover the common mistakes I've noticed among newbie traders.

Making mistakes is part of being human, and, for the most part, mistakes are inevitable. This is especially true if you're starting something new. If you're riding a bike for the first time, chances are you'll stumble and fall a few times. If you're learning how to draw, you'll probably make mistakes because you're not accustomed to the techniques and know-how that come with practice.

The same goes for trading.

If you're a newbie trader, chances are that you're going to make mistakes. However, unlike with drawing or riding a bike, you won't just walk away with a scraped knee or a poorly drawn picture. If you make a mistake in trade, you could lose money.

While mistakes are inevitable, there are a few

common mistakes that beginner traders make that are easily avoidable with a bit of caution and knowledge.

Lack of Preparation

Unlike with other hobbies or interests, you can't simply create a trading account and jump into live trading without any prior knowledge or experience. The risk of major losses is high if you go ahead without doing any groundwork. While this might be okay if you're loaded, for most of us, money is tight.

Therefore, if you want to begin and succeed in trade, you'll have to have some measure of discipline. You'll have to do your research and try to learn as much about trading as you can before jumping in. In addition to that, there are a plethora of skills that you'll have to pick up before you're ready.

We've mentioned the skills you'll need to learn in Chapter 2, but let's do a quick recap. The key skills you'll need to learn include things like knowing how to read market trends, knowing how to operate online trade platforms, having a working knowledge of how trade works, such as when to exit and enter positions, when and how to trade, and which financial instruments are ideal for you and your circumstances.

In addition to forgoing the research and practice aspects of trading, we've also noticed that, when entering the world of trade, most beginners are completely unaware of how much work goes into it. With trading, there are watchlists to create and track in order to know when and where to trade. You'll need to set up charting systems to track your portfolio, not to mention trying to implement a trading strategy.

With algorithmic trading, the learning curve and requirements are even steeper (see Chapter 2).

Not knowing when and how to properly execute trades or how to do your due diligence before trading will lead to growing losses. These losses are often easily avoidable.

Now, if you're reading this book, we're assuming you're one of the few who won't make this mistake. And to help you further your pre-trade prep, we've set up the next chapter, filled with additional resources to help you on your journey.

No Planning

This mistake goes hand in hand with the one mentioned above. After all, if you're not preparing, it's very unlikely that you've entered a trade with a solid trading strategy or plan.

You might jump into live trading with the sole aim of making money fast and rush to invest in stocks or assets that you think are on the rise without much thought behind the action. However, because you rushed in without a plan, the investments and trades you made could turn against you, and you'll start to incur losses. You might even lose all that you've invested and end up in a worse position than when you started.

Another aspect of this mistake is that you could've had a trading plan or strategy in mind but, due to excitement or impatience, you strayed from that plan and made some impulsive decisions.

Having a plan and not following through could cause the same losses as if you didn't have a plan at all.

Remember, one of the key tenets of being a trader is being patient and making deliberate, informed decisions when trading. If you're impulsive, impatient, and uninformed, it is highly unlikely that you'll succeed.

Allowing Emotions to Dictate Your Trades

Another mistake that goes hand in hand with the one mentioned above is human emotion. Now, emotions aren't inherently risky, nor do they inherently cause mistakes. However, once you allow your emotions to rule your actions without thought of the consequences of those actions, that's when it becomes an issue, especially within trading.

Every trader struggles to control their emotions and gut responses when trading. It's a constant push and pull as you battle with fear, confidence, and greed.

When starting out with trade, it's likely you'll be excited and ready to jump in and begin making money. On the other hand, you could feel scared and be cautious. And both these emotions are completely normal and natural.

In most cases, these emotions are a great way of motivating you. For example, fear helps you remain cautious and prevents you from being reckless and conducting risky trades. Greed could motivate you to work harder and learn more techniques and trade methods. Confidence can help you execute trades and enter and exit positions.

However, you should be careful not to let these emotions get the best of you.

Overconfidence and greed could cause you to take huge risks with your trades, while fear could prevent you from accessing trade opportunities.

What's important is to keep a cool head and stick to your trading plan for as long as it's serving you. If you need an outlet for those impulsive emotions, we would suggest you keep a paper trading account on hand to play around with.

Difficult and Complex Trading Patterns

On the opposite side of the spectrum to the trading mistakes we've covered thus far, are traders who've done their due diligence, have done the research, and have a comfortable working knowledge of how market exchanges and trading work.

With beginners who've done the groundwork and are confident in themselves, we've often seen the mistake of them choosing very complex, difficult trading strategies to start out with.

The problem with complex trading strategies is that they are often difficult to implement and require extensive experience as well as the skill set and knowledge to pull them off. Therefore, most beginners often find their trades and strategies failing because they lack the experience to make them work effectively.

In our experience, being successful at trade requires both experience and know-how. As excited and ready as you may be, we would caution against biting off more than you can chew.

Instead, start small with simple, easy-to-implement trade strategies until you find your feet. Once you're more comfortable and have gained more experience, you can branch out and experiment with more complex strategies.

Chapter 7:
Additional Resources

This chapter lists additional resources that you can use to learn more about algorithmic trading and upgrade your coding and trading skills.

We've split this chapter into two main sections. The first section focuses on trading and algorithmic trade specifically, while the second section focuses on building a trading computer and upgrading your coding skills.

Resources for (Algorithmic) Trade and Investment

In this section, we'll be covering resources that we think are ideal for beginners when starting their trading journey. If you'd like to learn more, we'd suggest you start here.

Udemy

Udemy is a great online learning resource that offers thousands of classes covering a wide variety of topics such as trading, investment, business management, and many others.

We found it quite impressive that these courses were created in collaboration with industry professionals. We think this drastically improved the quality and reliability of the courses. In this section, we've linked a very handy trading course that we think would suit beginners.

Not only is the course professionally curated, but the information is also delivered in a beginner-friendly, simple manner which I found enjoyable.

Udemy is a paid service. However, it is quite affordable and shouldn't break the bank. Once you pay for a specific course, you'll have lifetime access to that course as well as the ability to engage with instructors if you haven't understood the lesson well.

The only possible downside is that these courses don't offer diplomas or certificates. However, we don't think this should be much of an issue since the aim is to improve your trading skills.

The Disciplined Trader

The Disciplined Trader is an excellent beginner-friendly trading book that focuses on the psychology of trading and the mental discipline one needs if one wants to be successful.

While not the most recent book (published in 1990), we found it impressive that it has stood the test of time and is still considered by many to be a must-read.

Despite tackling a quite complex topic, we thought it was very simply written and easy to read. The author has done an amazing job at describing the basic mindset and attitudes that every trader should have.

We have included the Amazon link if you're interested in checking it out.

Algorithmic Trading & DMA

Algorithmic Trading and DMA is a book written by Barry Johnson that focuses on quantitative algorithmic trading. While a bit complex, we found this book incredibly useful when trying to wrap our heads around the complex concepts within algorithmic trading and coding.

The book focuses particularly on how market exchanges work and what Johnson termed the "market microstructure."

This book is essential if you want to learn more about how to create investment and trade strategies as well as get a handle on the inner workings of financial market exchanges.

Computer and Programming Resources

Finding reliable, beginner-friendly resources regarding coding and computers can be quite difficult. Now, we'll be the first to admit that we're not the most tech-savvy group of people, nor have we ever been very good with computers. So, when searching for resources to help build our programming and computer skills, we struggled to find ones that suited our beginner status.

Everything was either too complicated or not explained well enough. That being said, here are a few beginner-friendly resources that helped us out when we started as a team.

SkillShare

Now, if you've been on the internet for a while, we're sure you must've heard of skillshare by now.

Skillshare is an online learning platform that's ridiculously affordable at only $30 per year. It's a steal!

Skillshare offers thousands of courses that cover everything from photography to programming and coding. There are also various teachers on Skillshare, so if you're not into a certain class, you can almost always find another class on something similar.

The large variety of classes allows you to choose what suits you. In addition, Skillshare also allows you to choose when and where you'd like to learn. As long as you have a strong internet connection, the world is your oyster.

In this section, we've linked the Skillshare coding classes, which we think work well for beginners. You should also be able to find classes on trade and investment.

JayzTwoCents

Now, this is somewhat unconventional, but the YouTuber, JayzTwoCents, makes excellent videos about computers, computer components, and how to build a PC. He also does a ton of reviews on computer components such as motherboards, RAM cards, and power supplies.

When we stumbled across his channel, we found his instructions and explanations quite easy to follow and extremely user-friendly. His content is also very entertaining and professionally edited, and recorded. His videos are quite personal, and it often feels like speaking to a friend.

Much like with Skillshare, YouTube allows you to watch videos whenever and wherever you want, so long as you have access to the internet. This allows you the freedom to learn whenever you wish.

In addition to this, YouTube is completely free to use. There is a Premium version; however, we find this unnecessary.

The website also offers hundreds of thousands of other YouTube channels, some of which also cover trade and investment. We suggest you hit the search bar and explore these options.

Data Camp

Data Camp is another amazing online resource that specializes in coding and programming. Much like most of the resources on this list, there is a free version and a premium paid account; however, we haven't found that this has made much of a difference in our experience.

What we found quite great is that Data Camp offers a tutorial class called *'Python For Finance: Algorithmic Trading,'* which we think you'll find quite useful when building your coding skills. After all, while learning to code is essential, you'll also need to know how to translate a trading strategy into coding and how to do it effectively.

We found that this tutorial is great for learning how to code specifically for algorithmic trading. Not only is it beginner-friendly, but it's also completely online, which means you can learn when you want and where you want.

Once again, you'll have to have an internet connection if you'd like to access this resource.

Inside the Machine: An Illustrated Introduction to Microprocessors and Computer Architecture

This is a more traditional resource. The book *'Inside the Machine'* is a beginner's guide to computers and their various components.

Given that it's a beginner's guide, it's extremely user-friendly and uses simple language. We also found that it imparts information without overwhelming the reader or bombarding them with all kinds of complicated terms.

This book is aimed to help readers understand the basics of a modern computer and the different components of the computer. It also covers the basics of programming, including fundamental concepts and even some advanced lessons.

Overall, this is a great book to get you started in computers and programming, especially if you're a bit hesitant, given the technical nature of the subject.

Conclusion

And, just like that, we've reached the end of our journey together. Within the last few chapters, we've covered everything from the basics and requirements of algorithmic trading to risk management and algorithmic evaluation.

While we have tried our best to cram as much information into these chapters as humanly possible, we're afraid you've merely seen the tip of the iceberg.

As Chapter 7 demonstrated, there's a world of knowledge out there, and as you continue learning, you'll find that there is so much more that you don't know. Now, we don't mean to sound discouraging. If anything, we're hoping that our words will act as a motivator to push you onward toward greater things.

You picked up this book for a reason. It could've been simple interest, curiosity, or a desire to trade. Whatever your reason to pick it up, there is a reason you've stuck around until the very end. After all, no one forced you to finish it.

So, our question to you is, why did you stay? Curiosity only takes you so far, and we doubt it would sustain you for the length of an entire book.

If your answer is because you're truly interested in trading, then we're so glad to have had you.

As we've shown you, while trading isn't the easiest thing to pick up and master, it is possible. With the right tools at your disposal, we're sure you can reach your financial goals faster than you thought possible. All you need is patience and dedication.

As with all good things, being a master at trade and investments won't come easy. It certainly won't happen overnight. You'll have to put in the work, and it's going to be difficult, but we promise the rewards are worth it.

We can only hope that we've given you enough tools to get you started.

Now, you might be looking around wondering, what next? Where do I go from here?

Well, what happens next is entirely up to you. Your financial future is completely in your hands, and you decide where to go. You could choose to put this book away and forget all you've learned, or you could decide to pick up another finance book and equip yourself with more knowledge.

If you want to continue learning more about algorithmic trading and trade in general, Chapter 7 acts as a roadmap toward amazing resources that you can check out now that you've finished this book.

Before we see you off at the door, let us leave you with a few key takeaways, which we think sum up the lessons and information in this book pretty well. Think of it as a summary of what we've covered thus far.

Key Takeaways

In this section, we've compiled what we believe are the key tenets of the book. These are the key pieces of advice and information that we hope you'll carry with you, even if you end up forgetting everything else.

We've chosen a key tenet or takeaway from the chapters in this book to create something of a summary of lessons.

Know Your Basics

The first chapter of this book was pretty straightforward. It acted as an introduction or crash course in algorithmic trading. In many ways, it laid the foundation of what was to come.

That being said, we think that the best lesson you could learn from chapter one was to know the basics. This means being able to answer questions like *'What is algorithmic trading?', 'How does it work?',* and *'What are the advantages and disadvantages of algorithmic trading?'.*

You should also be familiar with the basics of trading, trade strategies, and how they work, as well as online brokers and the role they play in financial markets.

Now, you might be asking yourself why we're so adamant for you to know these things. Well, think of it this way: when building a house, you need a strong foundation, otherwise the house might collapse.

Knowing the basics of trade and investments is your foundation. It's what your trading journey will rest on as you grow and learn. If you're unclear about the basics, you could end up making simple mistakes that could cause you to lose money and have your trading career crash down around you.

Knowing the basics is so important because it offers you a sense of familiarity and direction. It helps you make important decisions like deciding which trading strategy to go with or which broker to choose.

Be Prepared

When starting any new venture or aspiring to a new goal, it's important to know what you'll need to get to where you want to be.

Let's say that you've been wanting to get into gardening. You've done all your reading, figured out the best soil type to grow your preferred flowers in and you've even found the best location in your home to start your garden.

While that's all fine and well, you can't actually start gardening until you've acquired all the necessary tools. These could be flower pots, seeds, watering cans, and soil.

Well, the same can be said about algorithmic trading. Having the basics committed to memory is great, but that alone doesn't make you an algorithmic trader. If you want to begin trading, you'll need the right tools.

Now, with manual trading, all you'll need is a good internet connection and a trading account with a broker to begin. However, as discussed in Chapter 2, you'll need a lot more than that to begin algorithmic trading.

The point here is to be prepared when entering a new venture, especially if it's something as complex as trading.

Consistency is Key

Once you've got your trading algorithm and account up and running according to the strategy you've chosen, it's not enough to just leave it alone and hope for the best.

While algorithmic trading is a form of automated trading, it still requires human intervention. It's not something you can set up and leave running.

Instead, you'll need to consistently monitor and evaluate the performance of your algorithm in order to ensure that it remains profitable and is able to keep up with market trends.

That being said, it isn't just your algorithm that needs constant maintenance. It's important that you don't stop learning and trying to improve your skills. After all, practice makes perfect.

So, we would recommend that, even if you become comfortable with trading, you never stop researching new methods and exploring various investment and trade options. With algorithmic trading, you'll also have to keep up with your coding and programming skills.

In addition to this, due to the constantly fluctuating financial markets, it's also a good idea to maintain consistency in keeping up with financial news. This allows you to prepare for any market shifts that may occur.

Understand the Risks Involved

Let's go back to the gardening example.

Let's say you begin gardening. You've got the soil, the seeds, the right location, and a gorgeous watering can—everything you could possibly need to get started. And so, you get started with planting and sowing and everything else that goes along with gardening.

Over time, your plants sprout, and everything seems to be going well. Then, one day, you wake up to find your plants half-eaten and nearly dead. Nestled between your plants, you find little insects and snails, all of which have had a feast on your new plants.

All that hard work down the drain, and all because you forgot to become acquainted with the risks involved with gardening.

As with gardening, trading comes with its fair share of risks. Chapter 6 goes into great detail about the risks associated with algorithmic trading and how to safeguard against them.

Being aware of the risks involved with algorithmic trading is the best way to protect yourself from them.

That being said, as much as it's important to be aware of the risks involved, it is equally important to accept that risks are inherent in trade and investment.

Final Thoughts

Now that we've reached the very end of this book and we've imparted as much knowledge and advice that these pages allow, it's time for us to say goodbye.

You're on your own now, and whether you decide to pursue your interest in trading or go on as you have is completely up to you.

But we can't help but say these last words:

Do not let your time spent reading this book be in vain. Learn, explore, and put your knowledge and skills to use.

We wish you well on your trading journey.

References

6 Steps to Evaluate Your Trading Strategy for Optimal
    Performance. (2019). Futures Day Trading
    Strategies.
    https://optimusfutures.com/tradeblog/archives/steps-
    to-evaluate-trading-strategy

12 Top Tips for Monitoring Algo Trading. (2019). Eventus
    Systems.
    https://www.eventussystems.com/monitoring-algo-
    trading/

Algorithm Trading: Benefits and Risks. (2017). Finextra.
    https://www.finextra.com/blogposting/14351/algorithm
    -trading-benefits-amp-risks

Barone, A. (2020). Introduction to Momentum Trading.
    Investopedia.
    https://www.investopedia.com/trading/introduction-to-
    momentum-trading/

Bhagat, V., & Singh, A. (2018). Algorithmic Trading
    Strategies and Modelling Ideas. QuantInsti;
    QuantInsti. https://blog.quantinsti.com/algorithmic-
    trading-strategies/

Bloomenthal, A. (2019). What Is Arbitrage? Investopedia.
    https://www.investopedia.com/ask/answers/what-is-
    arbitrage/

Bryant, M. R. (n.d.). Stress Testing for Trading Strategy
    Robustness (article): Adaptrade Software.
    Www.adaptrade.com. Retrieved August 4, 2021, from

http://www.adaptrade.com/Newsletter/NL-StressTesting.htm

Burns, S. (2020). What is an Equity Curve? New Trader U. https://www.newtraderu.com/2020/04/12/what-is-an-equity-curve/

Chen, J. (2019a). Algorithmic Trading Definition. Investopedia. https://www.investopedia.com/terms/a/algorithmictrading.asp

Chen, J. (2019b). Modern Portfolio Theory (MPT). Investopedia. https://www.investopedia.com/terms/m/modernportfoliotheory.asp

Chen, J. (2019c). Rebalancing. Investopedia. https://www.investopedia.com/terms/r/rebalancing.asp

Chen, J. (2021). Understanding the Theory of Mean Reversion. Investopedia. https://www.investopedia.com/terms/m/meanreversion.asp

Davey, K. (2019). The Ultimate Guide To Successful Algorithmic Trading | Hacker Noon. Hackernoon.com. https://hackernoon.com/the-ultimate-guide-to-successful-algo-trading-15r31fl

Desai, K. (2016). 5 Simple Tips for Risk Management for Day Traders. Bulls on Wall Street. https://bullsonwallstreet.com/risk-management-101/

Fernando, J. (2019). How to Use the Sharpe Ratio to Analyze Portfolio Risk Versus Return. Investopedia. https://www.investopedia.com/terms/s/sharperatio.asp

Fernando, J. (2021). Volume Weighted Average Price (VWAP) Definition. Investopedia. https://www.investopedia.com/terms/v/vwap.asp

Folger, J. (2019). How to Read a Strategy Performance Report. Investopedia. https://www.investopedia.com/articles/fundamental-analysis/10/strategy-performance-reports.asp

Fundamental, Technical and Sentiment Analysis. (2018). Orbex Forex Trading Blog. https://www.orbex.com/blog/en/2018/05/fundamental-technical-and-sentiment-analysis

Hayes, A. (2019). Understanding Scenario Analysis. Investopedia. https://www.investopedia.com/terms/s/scenario_analysis.asp

Hayes, A. (2020). Implementation Shortfall. Investopedia. https://www.investopedia.com/terms/i/implementation-shortfall.asp

Johnston, M. (2021). Coding Your Own Algo-Trading Robot. Investopedia. https://www.investopedia.com/articles/active-trading/081315/how-code-your-own-algo-trading-robot.asp

Kuepper, J. (2019). Risk management techniques for active traders. Investopedia. https://www.investopedia.com/articles/trading/09/risk-management.asp

Laster, S. (n.d.). The Benefits Of Algorithmic Trading. Www.fxempire.com. Retrieved August 4, 2021, from https://www.fxempire.com/education/article/the-benefits-algorithmic-trading-397949

Louis. (2020). Best Algorithmic Trading Platforms 2021 | Trade Options With Me. Trade Options with Me. https://tradeoptionswithme.com/best-algo-trading-platforms/

Mitchell, C. (2021). How trading algorithms are created. Investopedia. https://www.investopedia.com/articles/active-trading/111214/how-trading-algorithms-are-created.asp

Percent of Volume (POV). (n.d.). Www.interactivebrokers.com. Retrieved August 16, 2021, from https://www.interactivebrokers.com/en/software/tws/usersguidebook/algos/fox_pov.htm

Planning and Executing Index Rebalance Trades | Ryedale. (2021). Www.ryedale.com. https://www.ryedale.com/insights/thought-leadership/planning-and-executing-index-rebalance-trades/

Samuelsson. (2019). Trading Computer Guide (Algo trading, Swingtrading and Daytrading). The Robust Trader. https://therobusttrader.com/trading-computer-algorithmic-swing-trading-and-daytrading/

Samuelsson. (2021). Does Algorithmic Trading Work? (With Steps to Make It Work For You!). TheRobustTrader. https://therobusttrader.com/does-algorithmic-trading-work/

Seth, S. (2021a). Basics of Algorithmic Trading: Concepts and Examples. Investopedia. https://www.investopedia.com/articles/active-trading/101014/basics-algorithmic-trading-concepts-and-examples.asp

Seth, S. (2021b). Pick the Right Algorithmic Trading Software. Investopedia. https://www.investopedia.com/articles/active-trading/090815/picking-right-algorithmic-trading-software.asp

Sharma, R. (2021). Quantitative Trading Definition. Investopedia. https://www.investopedia.com/terms/q/quantitative-trading.asp

Smigel, L. (2019). Algorithmic Trading: Is It Worth It? Analyzing Alpha. https://analyzingalpha.com/algorithmic-trading-is-it-worth-it

Smith, T. (2019). Market Sentiment Definition. Investopedia. https://www.investopedia.com/terms/m/marketsentiment.asp

Solanki, J. (2020). Automated trading vs. manual trading. Admirals. https://admiralmarkets.com/education/articles/automated-trading/automated-trading-vs-manual-trading

Thakar, C. (2020a). Introduction to Risk Management in Trading. QuantInsti. https://blog.quantinsti.com/trading-risk-management/

Thakar, C. (2020b). Time-Weighted Average Price (TWAP) in Financial Markets. QuantInsti. https://blog.quantinsti.com/twap/

Trading Platform - Definition, What is Trading Platform, Advantages of Trading Platform, and Latest News. (2021). Cleartax.in. https://cleartax.in/g/terms/trading-platform

Printed by BoD"in Norderstedt, Germany